Contents

Introduction *vi*

1 The service sector
The shift to the service sector *1*
Regional variations in the location of service employment *3*
Shops and offices within the service sector *6*
Intra-urban locational trends *6*
Service-dominated cities *7*
Brussels—a service capital *8*
Summary *8*
Assignments *8*

2 The process of location
Conventional urban land use theory *11*
The property market *14*
Summary *18*
Assignments *18*

3 Retailing change in Europe
Structural differences in European retailing *19*
The decline in the number of retail outlets *20*
The rationalisation of retailing—high street mergers *21*
The internationalisation of retailing—the new European traders *22*
From supermarkets to hypermarkets *23*
The varying pace of change towards decentralised retailing *24*
Planning controls on hypermarkets and superstores *25*
Convenience stores *27*
Other large-scale shopping developments *27*
Regional shopping centres *27*
Brent Cross—a regional shopping centre in Britain *30*
Eastgate Centre, Basildon—the extension of an existing centre *30*
Summary *34*
Assignments *34*

4 Offices in European cities
Centralisation/deconcentration   35
Office location trends   36
Emerging patterns of office location   37
Summary   44
Assignments   45

5 The service sector and new technology
The pace of change   47
The electronic office   47
New technology in retailing   48
The future   51
The implications of new technology in shops and offices 51
Assignments   52

6 Shops and offices—where next?
The future of the office   53
The future of the shop   53
Locational change   54
Assignments   55

Conclusion   56

References   57

Index   58

Acknowledgements

Many companies, organisations and people have provided information which has been directly or indirectly useful in the writing of this book. I am indebted to all of them and particularly to the Commission for New Towns, Marks and Spencer plc, The Hammerson Group, Centre–File Limited, ASDA plc, Tesco Stores Ltd and Storehouse plc. I would also like to acknowledge the assistance of Yvonne Court, Alan Hallsworth and Ian Mayfield for supplying detailed information so willingly when requested. I am especially indebted to Professor John Dawson, and to the editors of this series, Hilary Winchester and David Pickard for their very helpful comments on an early draft of this book. I would like to thank Rosemary Shearer, who drew the majority of the maps in this book.

Data for Figures and Tables is taken from the following sources:
Bateman, 1985 (Reprinted by permission of Croom Helm) (Figure 24); Bennison, D. and Davies, R. L., 1977 (Figures 20 and 21); Burtenshaw *et al.*, 1981 (Reprinted by permission of John Wiley & Sons Ltd) (Figure 11); Commission for New Towns (Figures 18a, 18b and 19); Dawson *et al.*, 1983 (Table 5); *Estates Gazette*, 1 October 1983 (Table 3); Marquand, 1983 (Figure 3); National Accounts ESA, Eurostat, 1986 (Table 1); *Retail Trade International 1986*, Vol. 1 (Table 4).

I would like to thank the following for permission to reproduce their photographs:
Neil Bateman (p. 27); the Commission for New Towns (p. 30); Alistair Duncan (p. 49); A. G. Hallsworth (pp. 24 and 30); IBM (UK) (p. 36 and cover, bottom); London Docklands Development Corporation (p. 43 and cover, top left); Photo Agence d'Urbanisme de la Courly (p. 39); St Martin's Property Investment Ltd. (p. 43); L. Shurmer-Smith (p. 24); Southend Air Photography Photovideo Studio (p. 31). All other photographs (including the cover, top right) were taken by the author.

I am grateful to the following examination boards for permission to reproduce copyright material:
the Associated Examining Board; the Joint Matriculation Board; the University of Cambridge Local Examinations Syndicate; the Oxford and Cambridge Schools Examination Board; the University of London School Examinations Board.

Introduction

As western economies have become increasingly dependent upon the service sector, the attention of geographers has turned to a detailed analysis of service-based activities. Within this sector, shops and offices are both major employers and users of land, but they have been subjected to major locational changes in the last two decades. Hypermarkets and superstores are now almost commonplace, whilst business parks are being developed to offer an alternative location to the city centre. New technology in a variety of forms has the potential to revolutionise the service sector, both in terms of its operation and its location.

This book examines the service sector in general, but concentrates on the changes which have occurred in the shop and office sectors of Britain and its close neighbours in the EEC. Whilst not all countries have responded in the same way to the new pressures, there are some common features, including a move towards the decentralisation of facilities and an increased scale of operation in the service sector. The book includes numerous case studies, which document in detail the changes which are under consideration.

The development process leading to the building of new shops and offices is examined in Chapter 2. Chapters 3 and 4 document the major locational changes which shops and offices have been undergoing in European cities. New technology, which could fundamentally alter the pattern of urban activities for decades to come, is considered in Chapter 5. Chapter 6 looks at the future for shops and offices.

1
The service sector

Shops and offices are vital elements of the modern city. In most towns and cities, they are often distinctive landmarks either towering above the skyline, or dominating the main streets of the centre. Not only are they visually dominant, they are also vital centres of activity, forming the hub of the commercial life of the city. They are important centres of employment, especially as fewer people are now employed in manufacturing compared to those who provide services of one form or another. Recently, however, they have become even more significant as important changes have taken place both in the way in which they operate and where they are located.

Many of these changes are part of the wider locational processes which have altered the spatial patterns of activities within cities, with an increasing trend towards the decentralisation of first people and then functions away from the centre of the city. Others owe more to the structure of the retail trade, which has seen the introduction of progressively larger shops as retailers have competed with each other to gain larger shares of the available trade. Still other changes can be seen as a response of companies to the locational freedom brought by new technology, particularly in the fields of computers and telecommunications. This means, for example, that not all offices now need to be located in the city centre, but instead may be located in more pleasant surroundings, well away from the traditional areas of intensive commercial activity.

In this book many of these changes are considered, with particular attention being paid to Britain and its close neighbours in the EEC, especially France. Not only has retailing innovation been rapid in these countries in the last two decades but few large cities have escaped the attentions of office developers. At the same time, there are some important differences in the extent to which changes have affected European countries. This variation will emerge from a closer analysis of many of the examples discussed.

The shift to the service sector

Modern economies are highly dependent on what is usually termed the *service sector*. Translated into bricks and mortar—or more often concrete, steel and glass—this has meant that new buildings have had to be built to house the growing number of people who are engaged in service occupations of all sorts. While the wealth of cities and nations during the Industrial Revolution was founded on manufacturing located in factories, the twentieth century has seen the growth of services at a rate which has been quite unprecedented. With this change, it is the office block, not the factory which has become the symbol of a city's prosperity. A skyline of modern office blocks is a surer sign of growth and development than a vista of factory chimneys. There is no denying, of course, that manufacturing is still vitally important to the economies of countries such as Britain, France and West Germany, but no longer is it the only major source of wealth for these advanced economies, nor is it any longer the most important major employer of their labour. There has been a gradual transition from the dominance of activities which extracted and processed raw materials into manufactured goods—the primary and secondary sectors, through to services or the tertiary sector and beyond. To understand this fully, some definitions are needed.

Primary activities may be defined as those which directly exploit the earth's resources. Included in this category are agriculture, mining, forestry and fishing. *Secondary activities* are those which involve the processing of raw materials in some way. Manufacturing, therefore is a secondary activity. The *tertiary sector* of the economy includes the services which are provided for a population, either supporting the manufacturing sector, or offering services directly to the general public. By this rather broad definition, insurance companies and banks, offering services to manufacturing, business and private individuals, are part of the tertiary sector, but so too are retailers such as Marks and Spencer or Sainsbury.

The tertiary sector is a complex one, therefore, and the classification of economic activities has been extended to draw a distinction between some of the very varied activities which are included within it (see Figure 1). Thus transport and utilities have been seen as the tertiary sector, with insurance, finance, real estate and trade included in a *quaternary sector* and

Figure 1 Sectors of economic activity

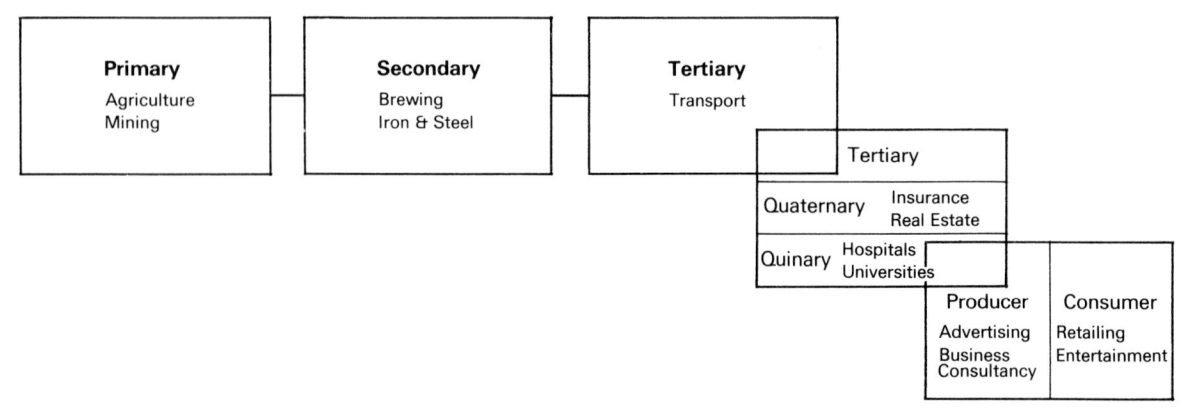

the higher level services of education, health, government, research, etc., being classified as a *quinary sector* (Gottmann, 1970; Bell, 1973; Daniels, 1982).

A further distinction can be made within the service sector between *producer services* and *consumer services*. The former are primarily those which are supporting the primary and secondary sectors, such as advertising agencies, engineering consultants and business services. Consumer services, on the other hand, are offered to the general public for direct consumption. They include a wide range of functions from retailing and entertainment to schools and health services. In practice it is not always easy to determine the division between producer services and consumer services. Even a brief consideration of the transport industry, for example, indicates clearly that a part of it, such as the London bus and underground train services, are consumer services; freight haulage, on the other hand, is a producer service. British Rail is an example of a service which is a mixture of the two. The distinction in the world of finance and insurance is an even more complex one and much more difficult to make—the National Westminster and the Midland Banks, for instance, offer their services to multinational companies and students alike.

There is no doubting, however, the growing importance of producer services to major western economies. Daniels estimates that some 22% of Britain's total workforce is now employed in producer services (Daniels, 1985). The recent growth of financial services, computing–related services and other services to the business community in general has been very rapid and accounts for much of the growth in the office sector.

Consumer services can be further sub-divided to distinguish between public and private services. The former includes hospitals, schools, and both local and national government departments. They are all essentially non-profit making services. Private services encompass those which are 'market services', or those which need contact with the public in order to sell their services.

The drift away from manufacturing employment towards services has been termed *de-industrialisation* and is one of the most important processes to have affected western societies in recent years. In the context of western Europe, there is some variation in the extent to which de-industrialisation has operated, but as Table 1 indicates, all countries show the trend to some degree.

In Britain, the share of the employed population in services rose from just over a half in 1951 to nearly two thirds in the early 1980s. Even Italy, one of the less advanced countries in the EEC had more than half of its employed population in the service sector, although it has always had a smaller proportion of its population in manufacturing industry, with a proportionately larger share of the population still working in agriculture. France, on the other hand, like Britain, has well over half of its working population employed in the service sector.

It should be noted that both the labour and capital productivity of the primary and secondary sectors has increased vastly during this period, with fewer people required to work on the land or in factories as increased production has been obtained by using more machinery and less labour. To some extent this has also happened in the service sector, but as yet the effect of automation has not been as great on employment in this sector as in the primary and secondary sectors. That is not to say that similar effects are not likely to occur; indeed major technological innovations may have far-reaching consequences. The current trends and possible effects will be considered in more detail in the last two chapters of this book. The overall effect of the changes so far, however, has been that services have become firmly established as the major employers in

Table 1 Percentage of the occupied population in each employment sector in selected member states of the EEC, 1970–1984

		B	D	DK	F	I	L	NL	UK
Agriculture, forestry & fishery prods.	1970	4.9	11.4	8.5	13.2	18.2	9.3	7.0	3.0
	1984	2.9	7.2	5.4	7.8	11.5	4.8	6.0	2.6
Fuel & power prods.	1970	2.1	0.6	2.0	1.6	0.9	1.0	1.2	3.2
	1984	1.5	0.7	1.9	1.5	0.9	0.9	1.4	2.5
Manufactured products	1970	30.4	25.0	36.6	26.4	27.7	33.2	26.2	33.5
	1984	21.7	19.4	29.9	22.7	24.3	25.7	19.0	23.1
Building & construction	1970	8.5	9.7	8.9	9.6	10.3	9.9	10.6	6.3
	1984	5.6	6.1	7.8	7.4	7.8	9.9	7.3	6.3
Market services	1970	36.9	34.5	30.4	32.8	28.8	35.9	41.5	36.8
	1984	45.7	34.7	35.4	41.1	37.2	45.9	49.2	44.6
Non-market services	1970	17.2	18.8	13.6	16.5	14.2	10.7	13.5	17.1
	1984	22.4	31.5	19.4	19.6	18.3	12.8	17.1	20.9

Key:
B Belgium
D W. Germany
DK Denmark
F France
I Italy
L Luxembourg
NL Netherlands
UK United Kingdom

advanced economies—a trend which still appears to be increasing. The current balance of employment in all the countries of the EEC is shown diagrammatically in Figure 2.

Regional variations in the location of service employment

The distinction which was made earlier between consumer and producer services is important when their location is considered. As the name implies, consumer services have to be located at points which are accessible to the consumer. This is true of both market services, such as retail outlets and public or state services, such as job centres or post offices. Broadly, therefore, consumer services are distributed on a regional scale approximately in proportion to the population. That is not to say that some parts of Britain are not better served than others, but simply that consumer services are provided to serve a local population.

Producer services have different constraints on their choice of location. They are not obliged to be close at hand to the consumer which they serve, but they do have to operate profitably. To do this, they need to attract good, well-qualified staff and may need to be located close to particular centres where information and research is located. For instance, a company developing computer software for engineering firms to assist their computer-aided design may in theory be located anywhere in the country, especially with the excellent communication facilities which are now available. In practice, however, such a company would need to be able to recruit software engineers and others, who would need considerable incentives to move to those parts of the country which are in economic decline. The reality of this industry is that many firms have chosen to locate along the M4 corridor stretching westwards from London, where employees can keep in touch with developments in their field by contacts with other companies. The area has acquired a reputation for such activity and provides what may be termed an *information-rich environment*, in which a great deal of research and development activity is going on. This also means that for the qualified software engineer, there are job opportunities available in a variety of firms in the computing field. The environment is an attractive one in which to live, which in itself ensures that suitably qualified people are willing to work there.

At a national scale, this means that employment in producer services is by no means evenly distributed. In Britain, Marquand has shown that service employment has grown particularly rapidly in areas outside the major conurbations, with strong growth being within 100 miles of London (Marquand, 1983). The case of employment change during the 1970s in insurance, banking and financial services is illustrated

Figure 2 Sectoral division of employment in all countries in the EEC in 1985

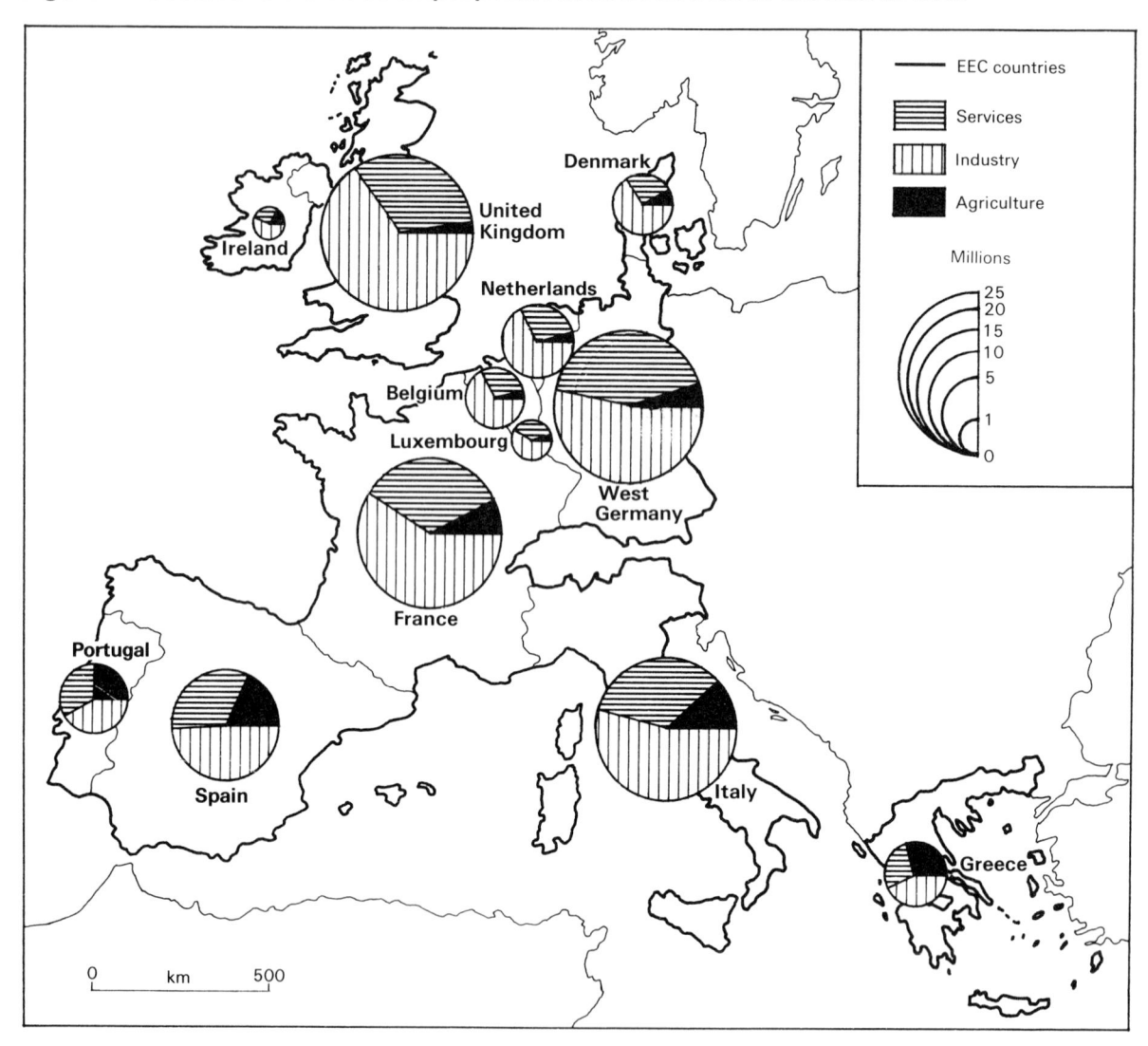

in Figure 3, where these trends are well marked. This pattern of change may seem surprising, but the major conurbations were not growing at the same rate as the smaller towns on their outskirts—a trend which has been noticeable in every major conurbation in Europe for the last 20 years.

In France, the disequilibrium between the Paris region (known as the *Ile de France*), and the rest of the country in terms of service employment has been recognised for many years. Indeed the French government has attempted to correct the imbalance through various planning policies, including the introduction of the *Métropoles d'Equilibre*, announced in 1965 primarily as a way of directing tertiary employment into the provinces (see Figure 4). Eight major provincial cities or groupings of urban centres were designated as growth centres to encourage the location of tertiary employment. This attempt at shifting the emphasis away from Paris was especially important in a country where the capital dominated all aspects of French life, including its administration of both the public and private sectors.

However, attempts to redirect the location of the service sector at a national level have never met with much success. To achieve their aims such policies have to include both national government and private companies in a system of controls on expansion in areas of growth, in favour of incentives to develop elsewhere. In the case of France, few companies accepted the incentives offered and the *Métropoles d'Equilibre* policy was superseded by a new policy in 1972. This favoured assistance to medium-sized cities

Figure 3 Changes in the distribution of employment in insurance, banking and financial services in Great Britain, 1971–77

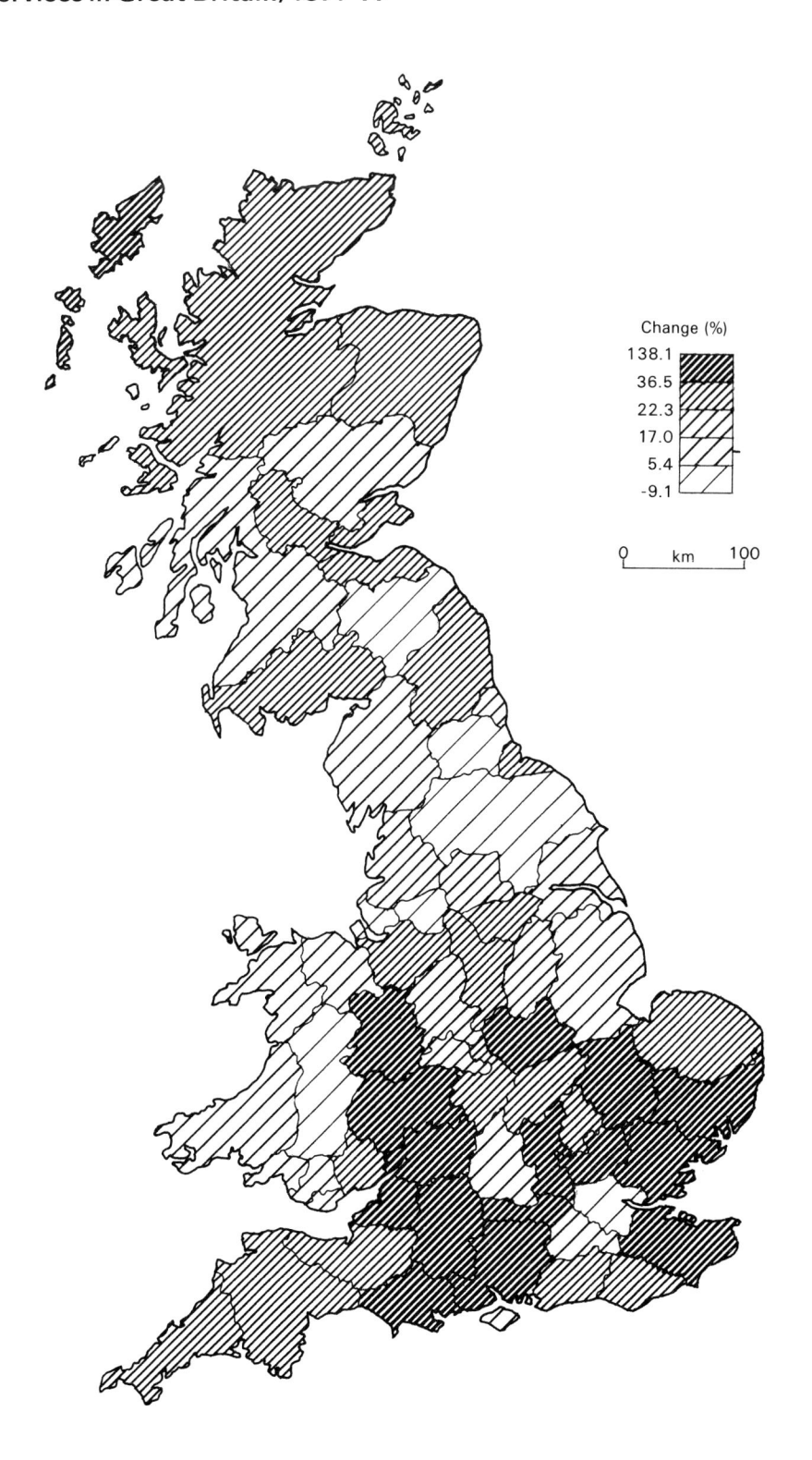

Figure 4 France: Métropoles d'Equilibre (1965)

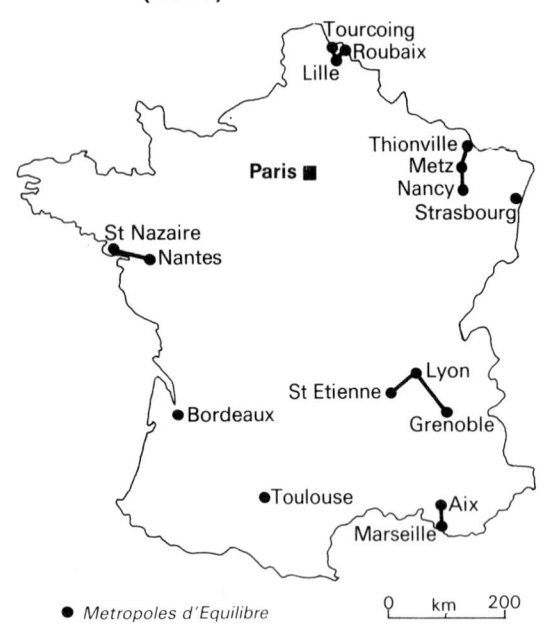

• Métropoles d'Equilibre

and towns, with populations between 50,000 and 200,000 throughout France, rather than merely channelling growth into the major provincial centres. In effect, only direct action by governments to relocate their own office jobs has really met with any success and even this has usually been on a modest scale. In Britain, two examples are the moves by the Department of Health and Social Security to Newcastle-upon-Tyne and the DVLC (Driving and Vehicle Licensing Centre) to Swansea in South Wales.

The result of this regional imbalance is that office jobs are unevenly distributed. In turn, this has meant that not all major cities and their surrounding metropolitan areas have been subjected to the same growth pressures. In most countries, it is the capital city, such as London, Paris and Brussels, which has felt most strain. In both the Netherlands and West Germany, however, the relatively small size of their capital cities has meant that this is not the case. Their major centres of commercial activity are not in the Hague or Bonn, but in Amsterdam and Rotterdam, and in Frankfurt and Dusseldorf. In these countries, it is these non-capital cities which have been more affected by the strains of providing space for the growing number of offices.

Shops and offices within the service sector

In this book, attention is focussed on retailing and the office sector, rather than on the whole of the service sector since that would include not only shops and offices but also non-office based government services such as schools and hospitals, as well as activities such as recreation and entertainment. Both retailing and offices are major users of land in cities. Furthermore, they have been the subject of planning control at a number of levels in many European countries. Both have seen major changes in their organisation and management, their scale of operation, the type of buildings in which they are sited and their location within the city. One of the most important locational changes which has affected the city has been caused by the movement of activities from the centre to the suburb.

Intra-urban locational trends

At the heart of the locational processes which have affected shops and offices are the twin but opposing trends of centralisation and dispersal. Cities grew by attracting people and functions, providing a forum where both information and goods could be exchanged. Over time, urban functions became concentrated in one place; contact with potential customers or with clients brought traders and commerce into the growing city, creating the major metropolitan centres which are present today. Cities in western societies came to be characterised by city centres which contained the major retail stores with offices in close proximity. Both essentially sought the *accessibility* offered by the city. As public transport became well developed, the wealthier sections of the community could live at greater and greater distances from the city centre, yet still avail themselves of its services as and when they required. A central location was frequently seen as essential by office users who valued the *contact environment* created by being close to other branches of commerce or to offices within the city. Department stores and major chain stores were at the most accessible locations in the city and could draw in their customers from the suburbs and beyond without difficulty. This situation existed in cities in Europe from the late nineteenth century until the 1960s when other locational trends began to exert themselves—echoing what had already begun in North America at least a decade earlier.

The rise in personal mobility which came with increase in car ownership enabled the new process of dispersal to take place. Without that increase in mobility, companies were not able to move any activities away from the centre, even though for many concerns, major economies could be made by operating on a large scale in a suburban location where land and other costs were cheaper. Once private transport became commonplace and, more significantly, once people expected to use their car for shopping, other locations away from the city centre became more accessible and by the 1960s, retailers had begun to cater for this demand. New forms of shops began to appear—superstores, hypermarkets and sometimes complete shopping centres, with department stores, and the various types of shop which one would normally expect to find in the city centre. The extent to which these trends affected the various countries in western Europe will be examined in more detail in Chapter 3, but it can be stated generally that by the late 1960s the trend towards concentration had begun to be reversed. Moreover, by the 1980s the trend towards dispersal was well established. The major factor which prevented even greater dispersal was the controls which were placed on it by planning policies – sometimes by national government and sometimes at the local level.

The second factor which enabled the dispersal of offices, following that of shops, was the tremendous improvement in communications technology, which often rendered face-to-face contact far less important than it had been previously. In effect new communications technology brought about the mobility of information, in much the same way that developments in transport technology had given rise to the mobility of people. It is arguable how much personal or face-to-face contact actually took place compared to contact by telephone. Nonetheless, it was certainly evident by the beginning of the 1980s that many business concerns had become convinced that they could move some, if not all, of their activities from the high value sites of the city centres. They could move either to the suburbs or to the medium-sized towns of the outer zones of the metropolitan areas of major cities. In London, for example, offices were able to move from the City of London or the West End to locations such as Croydon, Guildford or Reading, leaving the central locations to those offices which still needed the close proximity of other businesses. The extent to which modern developments in communications technology are likely to affect the location of offices still further will be considered in Chapter 5. It should be noted at this stage, however, that current communications systems which allow the transfer of information, data and even visual images from one place to another make it possible in theory for an office to be located anywhere in a country—or indeed in the world—and still enjoy the contact with other businesses which was previously only possible if they were grouped closely together.

Whilst improvements in communications generally have allowed decentralisation to take place, there have been costs, as well as benefits arising from this process. It is possible to summarise the advantages

Table 2 The advantages and disadvantages of centralisation and decentralisation

	For	Against
Centralisation	1 Contact environment	1 Congestion
	2 Ease of access by public transport	2 High land prices
		3 Difficult to expand business
		4 Poor environment
Decentralisation	1 Land available	1 Loss of direct contact
	2 High environmental standards	2 Dependence on private transport
	3 Ease of access by private transport	3 Possible loss of open land
	4 Lower land prices	4 Disadvantages low paid/less mobile population
	5 Telecommunications provide good contact	

and disadvantages of centralised and decentralised locations. Some have already been discussed, but there are others which have a bearing on the desirability or otherwise of a large scale move out of the city to its outskirts.

Service-dominated cities

The growth of the service sector has been general throughout Europe. At the same time, some cities have been particularly affected by these trends towards service-dominated economies. The city of Paris by 1975 had over two thirds of its employed population in service occupations and by the 1982 Census, as much as 80% of its employed population earned their living in the service sector. London has seen a dramatic decline in its manufacturing employment in the last 20 years, losing as much as two thirds of its manufacturing jobs and leaving it even more dependent on the service sector. It is interesting to note that in London's former dockland areas, bordering the Thames, current and recent developments have almost always meant an increase in office jobs, rather than a replacement of any manufacturing or other manual service occupations which previously existed there. The demand for traditional manufacturing skills has declined very rapidly, with newer industry requiring less and often better qualified labour. Service jobs have been increasing, but this rise should not obscure the fact that there have been significant changes in the skills required by the service sector. For instance, while office jobs have continued to increase, different skills are now required from the traditional clerical skills needed 10 or 20 years ago.

In Europe, some cities have become centres of services at a number of scales. Not only are they important service centres for their surrounding regions, but they are also national and international centres, housing the administrations of government and international organisations. This has contributed to the expansion of cities such as Paris, Luxembourg and Geneva, but is probably best illustrated by the case of the Belgian capital, Brussels.

Brussels—a service capital

A quarter of all Belgian office employment is located in Brussels, with an even greater dominance of the country's finance and commerce. In the country as a whole there were particularly sharp increases in employment in finance and insurance during the early 1970s, when in a five year period from 1970 to 1975, the employment in these sectors doubled—from 93,000 to 189,000. Most of this growth was concentrated in the capital. Besides this growth of jobs in the private sector, however, there has been a considerable growth in the public sector, especially through the establishment and expansion of international organisations. The North Atlantic Treaty Organisation (NATO) established its headquarters there in 1968, but it is its European role which has created the greatest growth. As the home of the European Commission of the European Economic Community (EEC), (even though the European Parliament is in Strasbourg), Brussels has seen a very rapid development. The EEC employs 10,000 people within the capital—mostly in an area of the city surrounding the EEC headquarters to the east of the historic centre. In addition, the presence of the European Commission has drawn in other offices from both the private and public sectors. The private sector offices have been established by companies wishing either to set up their own European headquarters in the city or at least to have an office there. The public sector growth has included the establishment of offices by foreign governments who wish to have a presence in the city, given the importance of European trade. The result is that by 1984, the Belgian state occupied 35% of the six million square metres of office space in the city, and international organisations a further 15% (Lasserre, 1985). This left only half of the office space occupied by the private sector, and of that, almost half was occupied by foreign companies.

Summary

In this chapter, the central role of the service sector has been discussed. Shops and offices are important to modern economies, and service employment has become more important than employment in manufacturing. The service sector has distinct locational tendencies, but before a more detailed examination of these, Chapter 2 considers the development process which leads to the building of new shops and offices.

Assignments

1 Refer to Figure 2. Draw a triangular graph to illustrate the relative position of each of the EEC countries. While they are closely grouped in the graph, to what extent is it possible to classify the EEC countries using this information?
2 Examine this table of GDP per capita:
Belgium $7638, Denmark $9834, France $8115, Greece $2966, Ireland $4733, Italy $5549, Luxembourg $9289, Netherlands $7716, Portugal $2344, Spain $3853, U.K. $6514, W. Germany $9064 (figures for 1986). What is the degree of correlation between numbers employed in the tertiary sector and GDP per capita?

Questions from A level examination papers

3 Describe and account for the distribution and character of retailing in any ONE large city or town. (Associated Examining Board, June 1984)
4 Explain the recent rapid growth of the tertiary sector of employment. (London, June 1986)

2
The process of location

City centres are continually in a state of change. Old buildings are being replaced, while some traditional functions are forsaking the centre for other locations either elsewhere within the city or outside it. Even a casual visit to the central area of almost any of Europe's major cities will leave an impression of new building, including new office blocks, often multi-storeyed and faced in modern materials such as tinted glass, and new shopping centres which employ the very latest selling techniques in their quest for more customers. In some cities, the accent is on restoration and conservation, but even there, new types of shopping are being established—the takeaway fast-food outlet in all its forms has clearly arrived even in the most historic centres. Some buildings are restored or renovated, only to be given virtually brand new interiors housing new office and retailing technology. Of course change is not confined merely to the centre of the city, even though its visual impact may be particularly strong there. At the edge of cities throughout the EEC, vast new shopping centres or individual shops such as hypermarkets, have been established, as well as new office complexes, often in the form of landscaped business or office parks.

These changes are considered in more detail in the following chapters, but the process of change in itself raises a number of questions. First, why is this activity taking place and who is responsible for it? Who decides that a new shopping facility should be developed or that an office block should be built? Indeed, outside the city, what are the processes which lead to the development of out-of-town shopping centres or the landscaped business park? Behind all of this development, which is a part of what is termed *property development*, lies a complex decision-making process which involves financiers, developers, and planners as well as those who will eventually occupy the building. In this chapter this process will be explained so that the reasons for the changes which can seen in the city can be understood.

Within the total mix of urban land uses, the centre of a city has many shops and offices, a large number of which have been sited there for many years, intermingled with new developments from the recent past. The current pattern of land use also includes other buildings such as cinemas, town halls, and churches, as well as some residential buildings. It is the result of hundreds, if not thousands of decisions which have been taken in the past. In large cities, there will probably be a regularity in the pattern of city centre functions with, for instance, major stores in one particular area and offices in another. The land use picture will be a very complex one, and obviously it will vary from one city to another, but theories of urban land use location have been proposed which attempt to explain such patterns. A question which needs to be considered is whether these theories offer a reasonable explanation for the pattern which can be seen in the cities of western Europe today.

A further question relates to the development process itself. In today's city, this process and the decisions which trigger it are far more complex than those which operated in the city of a century ago. Then a retailer could set up business and sell goods from a store on the local high street. Similarly, a local bank could buy a site, erect a building sufficiently imposing to inspire confidence in potential depositors and conduct its business from its new premises. Only rarely in either case would it have been necessary to seek the permission of the local authority before commencing the building of the new premises. Usually this meant that individual building plots were developed in a piecemeal fashion, often preserving and reinforcing the patterns of ownership and development of the city which could be traced back to the Middle Ages. One owner would decide to sell land to a developer, followed successively by neighbours until the entire area was developed by commercial entrepreneurs. Of course the same process operates today on the edge of a city as residential developers, such as Wimpey or Barratt acquire fields or even whole farms and so shape the pattern of urban development. An excellent example of previous ownership patterns still preserved can be seen in the centre of Leeds, where the buildings and arcades lining the main shopping thoroughfare of Briggate still follow the plots of land ownership which existed prior to the commercial growth of the city. This is shown in Figure 5, where individual building plots are outlined. Today, while these plots are occupied by the shops of major high street retailers, their

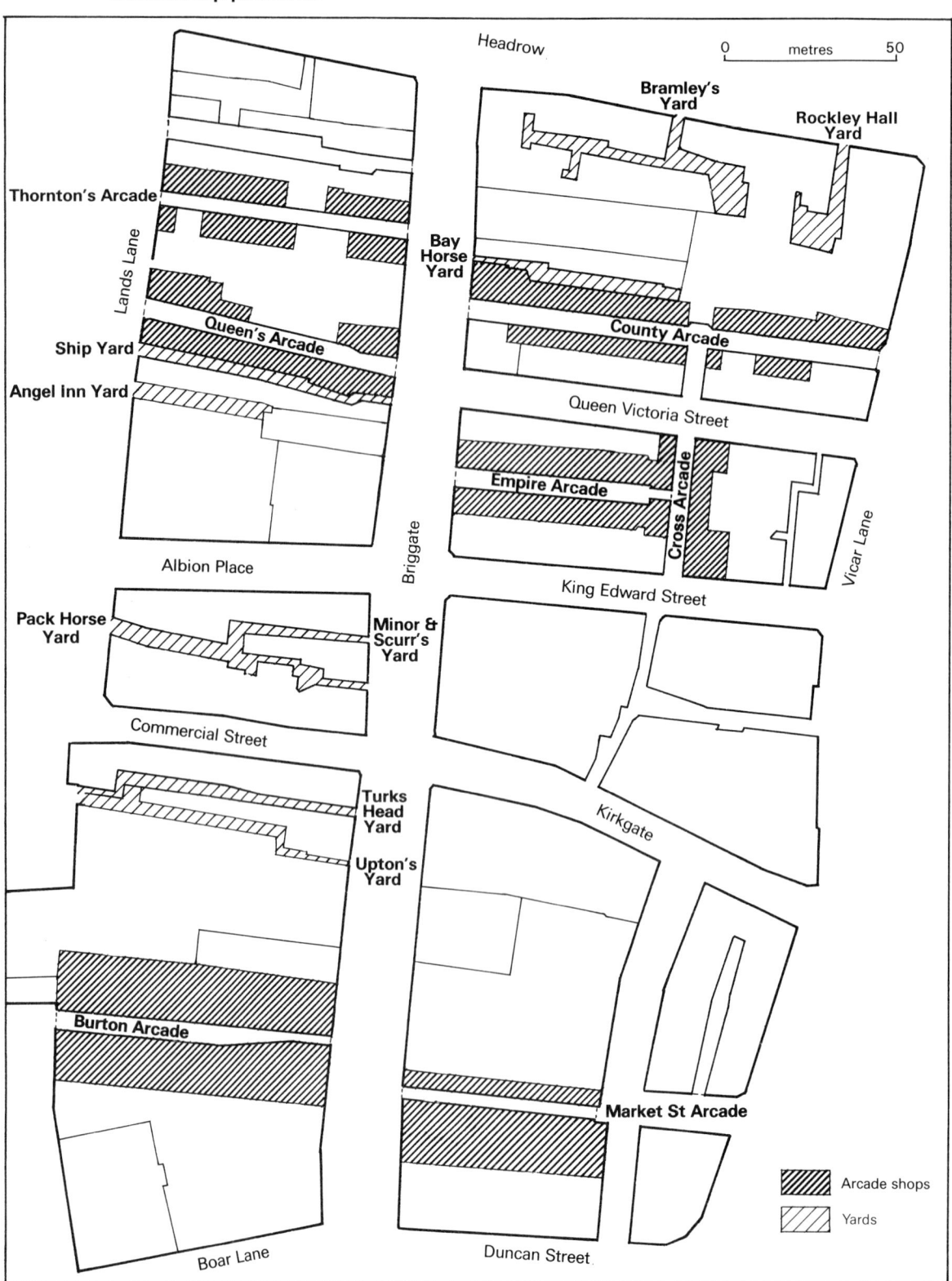

Figure 5 Briggate, Leeds, with alleyways and shopping arcades, reflecting previous land ownership patterns

physical shape was determined several hundred years ago.

In other cases, however, major redevelopment projects have involved not just single building plots but one or more entire street blocks, changing the street pattern quite markedly. These major redevelopment projects have been carried out by the property industry which has provided the finance and initiatives for these new developments. In this chapter, the industry will be examined in a little more detail, with the particular aim of discovering how the service sector is affected by it.

Conventional urban land use theory

One common factor shared by all services is that they must be sited where their customers or clients can reach them or where they can reach their customers with a minimum of cost and inconvenience. In other words, they require a degree of *accessibility*. This rather abstract word can be defined as the *potential for interaction*, or the likelihood of that location fostering contact (or interaction) between the service and its clients. Some locations will do this much more successfully than others. As long as people need to move to use the services, it is the transport network of the city which endows locations with their accessibility, the points of greatest accessibility being found where transport routes focus. In their turn, these accessible locations will be able to attract the greatest number of people—or potential customers or clients. It follows that not only are such sites more accessible, but they are also more valuable in terms either of the rent which has to be paid to the landlord, or the price which has to be paid to purchase the site.

While some sites are more accessible, it is equally important to note that some users of land, or occupiers of buildings require a higher level of accessibility than others. Familiar names in the British high street, such as W. H. Smith, Next, Habitat, Mothercare, Dixons and Marks and Spencer require a high degree of accessibility in order to attract a sufficiently large clientele to their stores to allow them to break even. In other words, they need to serve a market of a larger size than smaller retailers. In practice of course, the shareholders of such stores will require that they not only break even, but that they trade profitably from the site which has been selected. This tendency for large stores to serve market areas of a large size leads to an agglomeration or concentration of stores at those locations which are central to large market areas.

Other land uses, or even smaller, very specialised retailers, may not require these high levels of accessibility offered at the centre of large market areas, where they would not be willing to pay the high rents or land prices demanded. Some retailers of certain goods may seek the advantages of *agglomeration*, by clustering together in one area of the city centre. By grouping together, stores can offer the potential customer a wider choice of goods at one location than if they were dispersed about the city. Because of this, consumers are willing to travel a longer distance, which in effect means that the shops have extended their accessibility to a larger market. The effect of this is that at the centre of the city, groupings of stores such as clothing and shoe shops have often come to dominate some of the most accessible locations.

Retail clustering.

The notion of accessibility and the ideas which stem from it are the basis of *bid rent theory*, which suggests that land uses generally organise themselves in the city according to the value which the occupiers of land place on accessibility. Thus a department store, which requires a high level of accessibility, will outbid a solicitor, who may still require a site with a reasonable degree of access for his or her clients, but who will be unable to pay the highest prices needed to secure the most accessible sites in the city centre.

This sorting of land uses according to the value which is placed on accessibility can be thought of as a sort of land auction, where each use bids against all other uses for land, with each willing to pay a different price for land with a particular level of accessibility. The land use which bids the highest price (or rent) for the land will, at least in theory, occupy it. This is the essence of bid rent theory, which is shown diagrammatically in Figure 6. It is evident that some uses will gravitate towards the most accessible sites, which will themselves become the points of the highest land values as this hypothetical auction takes place. Two points need to be made, however, when we consider this model in detail. First, as was pointed out above, the accessibility pattern is determined by the transport pattern. For the greater part of this century, it was reasonable to suppose that the points of highest accessibility were in the centre of the city, where transport routes converge and to which most of the population had relatively easy access, especially by public transport. More recently, however, the building of urban motorways or freeways has produced a new pattern of accessibility in the city. Even new public transport systems, while focussed on the city centre, have frequently benefited not only the city centre, but also some suburban locations.

Figure 6 Bid rent theory—traditional view from the city centre

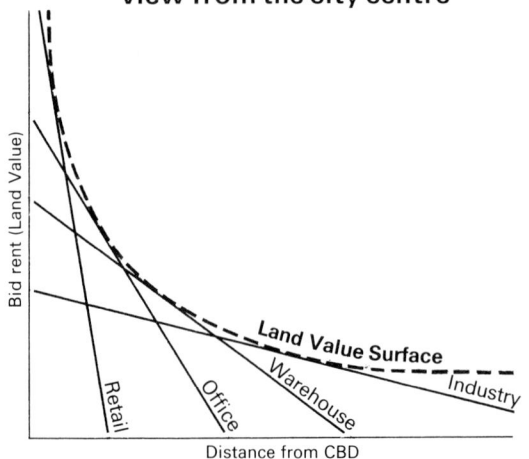

Meanwhile the city centre itself has been suffering from increasing congestion which has threatened to destroy the very accessibility on which so many of its functions depend. This has meant that the most accessible points are no longer automatically in the centre of the city, but perhaps at its periphery, in its suburban fringe and quite frequently where motorways or freeways meet. These then form the new peak accessibility points in the city and in the case of North American cities, the location of retailing has largely followed this new pattern of accessibility. The extension of the bid rent model to accommodate this new accessibility surface is shown in Figure 7.

Figure 7 Bid rent theory as it might be applied at a suburban point of high accessibility

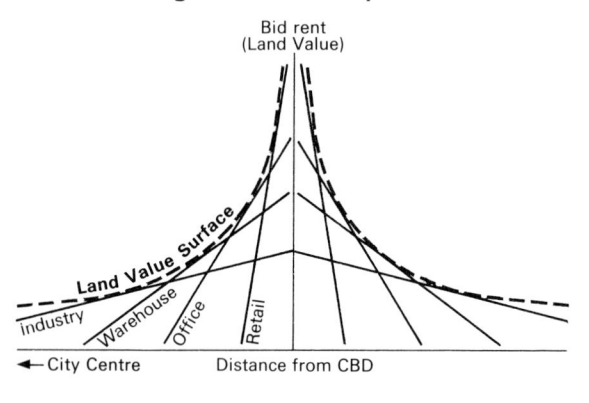

We will see in the following chapter that the extent of this trend towards a decentralisation of activities has varied widely from one country to another in western Europe. Quite plainly in the London region, however, the completion of the M25 orbital motorway, shown in Figure 8, has ensured that some locations, especially where other radiating motorways meet the M25, are extremely accessible. Already, offices have been developed close to the intersections of the major radial routes out of London, such as the M3 and M4 motorways and the M25. Plans are in existence for major retailing developments at points around the M25, as shown in Figure 8 and it seems inevitable that there will be major changes in land use in these areas during the next few years in response to this new pattern of accessibility.

The full impact of this new accessibility on the service structure of a city is best examined by looking not at a European city, but at one in North America. Figure 9 shows the pattern of out-of-town shopping centres in the Chicago region in the U.S., where the major department stores have become almost completely suburbanised, forsaking their traditional city centre location and becoming integral parts of out-of-town shopping centres. No European city has seen its retailing suburbanised on the scale of North American cities, although the development of some of these trends has been much more widespread in countries in mainland Europe than in Britain, as will be seen in the following chapter.

Although bid rent theory has had to be modified to accommodate the new accessibility surface of the city, it still offers a general level of explanation for the location of services in the city. The fact remains, however, that cities do not have strictly regular patterns of land value and use. Instead, they are a reflection of locational decisions which although they may have been made within the general framework of

Figure 8 The motorway pattern around London, showing proposals for new regional shopping centres

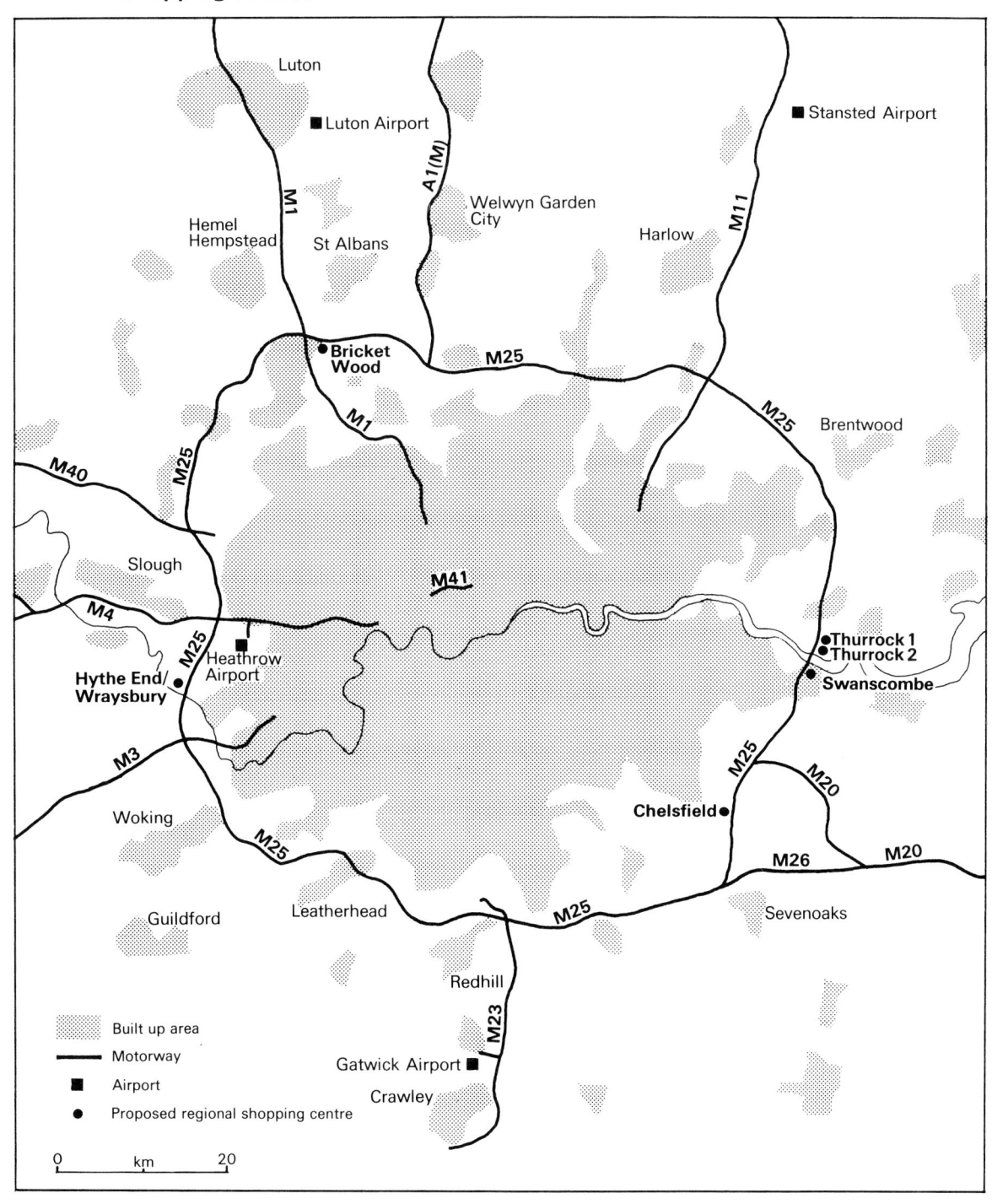

bid rent theory, will probably have been influenced by many other factors too.

Some of these factors will be historical since an examination of any European city will indicate that its land use pattern is the result of historical evolution, which has left its mark in the form of historic buildings, such as churches and other public buildings. The present city centre may then house not only shops and offices, but also royal palaces, cathedrals,

Figure 9 Regional shopping centres in the Chicago region

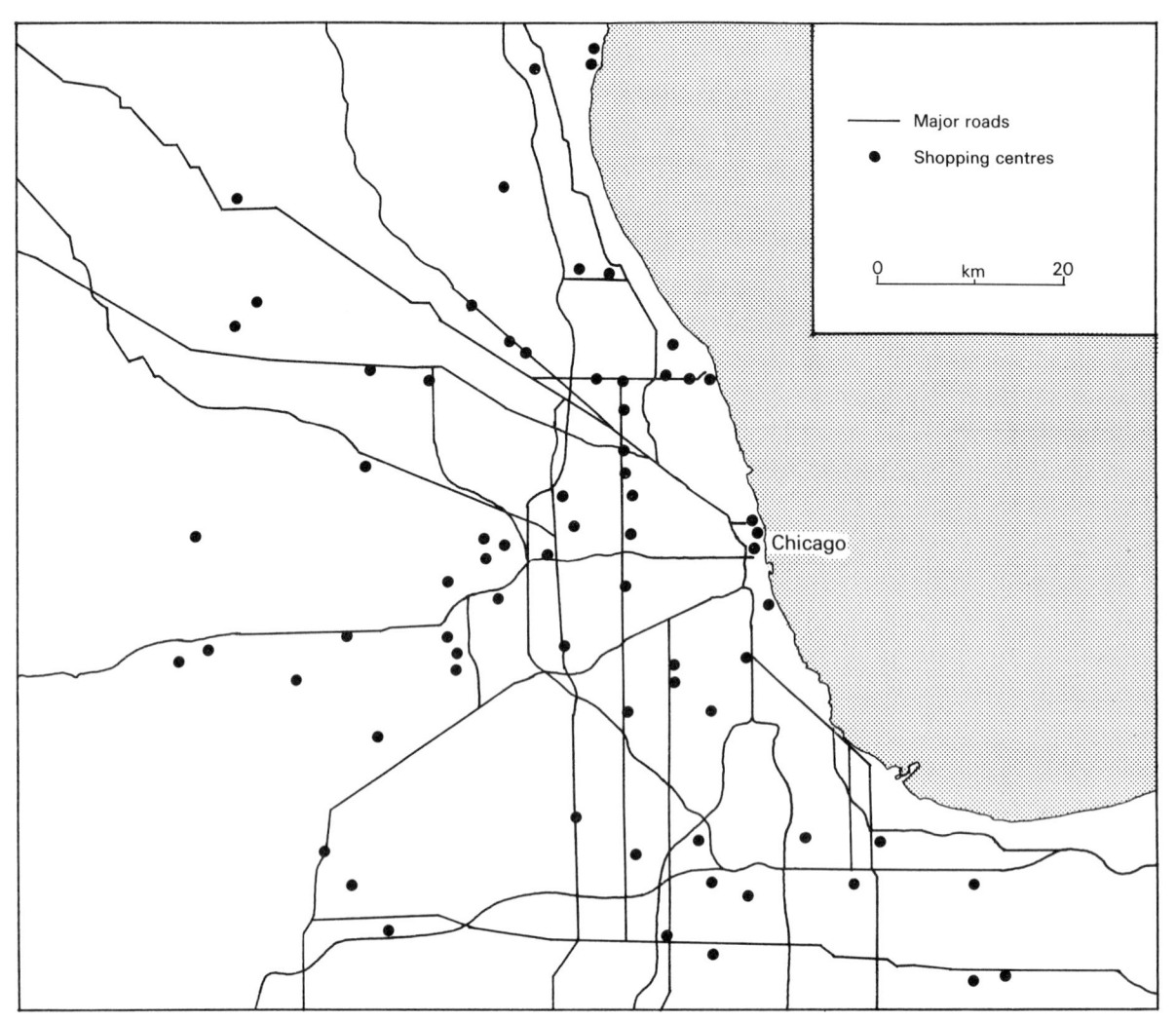

art galleries and many other buildings dating from a previous era. In many European cities, residential land use has continued to be important, even close to the commercial core—certainly to a far greater extent than has been the case in most British cities. In addition, since many commercial sites in the city are leased by the occupier for a particular period of time, rather than owned outright, land uses may not change until the expiry of that lease, often ensuring the survival of a business in a location where it would not otherwise be competitive in the modern land market.

Other factors which affect land values and use include individual site characteristics, associated land uses, or other uses in close proximity and the level of infrastructure which is provided. The urban land use pattern is, therefore, a complex one which can only be explained by a careful consideration of all the factors involved, both historical and current.

The property market

In any city, urban rent theory may well go some way to explaining the general pattern of land use, but the fact remains that detailed changes of land use are determined by the operation of the property market. An understanding of how property is developed will provide a greater understanding of the whole process of urban development, and especially of how shops and offices are developed within cities.

When any new building is developed, whether it is a shopping centre or an office complex, a number of people are involved in the decision to build it and who

Figure 10 The land development system

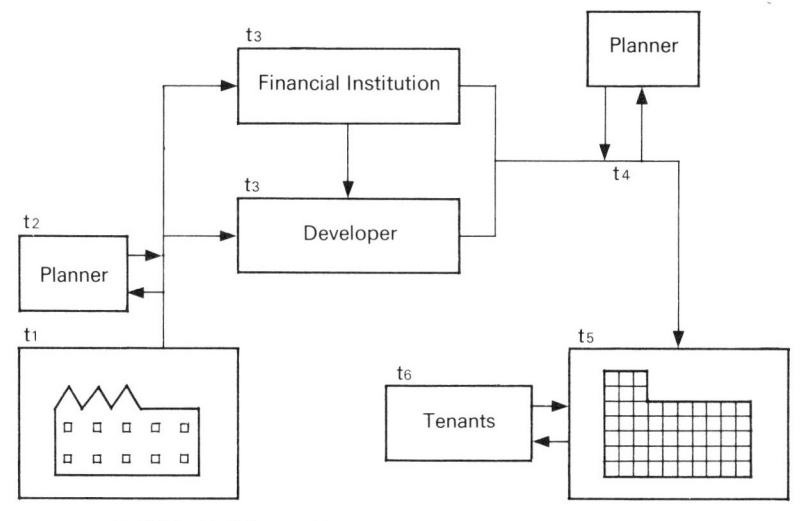

t1 Original buildings sold
t2 Plans submitted/modified
t3 Developer / Financial Institution - finance new building
t4 Plans submitted / modified
t5 Building completed
t6 Building occupied

NB Plans are submitted at either t2 or t4

eventually occupies it, as indicated in Figure 10. Those people primarily concerned with the development process are:
1 Financiers, who are responsible for providing the money to purchase the site and to construct the building.
2 Developers, who put forward a proposal for the building and who require the finance capital from the financiers.
3 Planners, who decide whether or not to grant planning permission for a particular building to be constructed.
4 Estate agents, who are responsible for obtaining tenants for the completed building.
5 Occupiers, who eventually move into the building.

This list does not include the company which actually constructs the office block or shopping centre, nor the architect who designs it. It also assumes that most new building is built as an investment, or as a speculative venture, and not simply built by a company for its own use. In practice, of course, some companies do build shops and offices for their own use, but many are built as an investment. Although the list above may suggest that each area of activity — finance, development etc. — is fairly separate, in practice this may not be the case. A close look at the current structure of Britain's property development industry will illustrate this.

Property developers and financial institutions

Twenty years ago, many of the centres of Britain's towns and cities were being redeveloped by *property development companies*. Large tracts of land were bought by a development company and redeveloped in major schemes, which included new shopping facilities, offices and often multi-storey car-parking. Examples included the St George's Centre in Preston, the Manders Centre in Wolverhampton, and on a larger scale, the Victoria Centre in Nottingham and the Eldon Square Centre in Newcastle-upon-Tyne. Property companies borrowed the money to pay for the developments from insurance companies and other financial institutions. A fall in the value of property in 1974–75 considerably reduced the number of property development companies in Britain — several in fact became bankrupt at that time, leaving only 105 still surviving in 1977, compared to 164 ten years earlier. Since then, the number of companies specialising in property has increased to 126, but the financial institutions themselves have begun to take a much more active and direct role in property development, rather than merely providing the finance for it.

Financial institutions include insurance companies, pension funds and banks, although it is the first two which have been the most active in property development. During the post-war period, two major social changes have meant that very large sums of money have become available to these institutions. There has been a considerable increase in life insurance business, which has produced large amounts of money from insurance premiums which have to be invested securely by the insurance companies, and there has been a growth of pension schemes linked to employment, creating very large pension funds. The result of both of these trends has been the creation of a huge amount of money available for investment, which in the case of Britain has been currently estimated at an annual sum of £3.6 billion.

Property has always been attractive to investors because in the long term it has proved to be a secure investment, which has performed well relative to other investments. Since pension funds and insurance companies are particularly interested in investments which offer long term security rather than short term but uncertain profit, property has always figured prominently in their investments. In broad terms, about one fifth of all their assets are in land and property. The final point to make in relation to their pattern of investments is that British financial institutions are by no means confined to ownership of British land and property. During the 1970s, many of them invested in European cities and from the end of that decade onwards they became increasingly interested in investment in cities further afield, especially in the U.S. The British Post Office Pension Fund owns an office block on the fashionable Rue de Rivoli in central Paris, which is tenanted by the French Ministry of Finance. The National Coal Board Pension Fund has major holdings in the U.S., including the Watergate complex in Washington DC. A glance at the advertising hoarding on any new development of shops, offices, business park or industrial estate will probably indicate the close involvement of one of the major financial institutions in the development.

A similar growth of investment finance has been apparent in European countries and there too, urban property has often been seen as a sensible investment. However, with the exception of the Dutch pension funds, the general patterns of investments have been different from their British counterparts, often funding residential rather than commercial property and sometimes having their freedom to invest abroad curtailed by law, as in the case of both the Swiss and West German pension funds.

Table 3 indicates the extent of the property investments held by the major British financial institutions.

Table 3 Investment by major British insurance companies and pension funds, 1983

	Total Investments (£m)	Property Holdings (£m)
Prudential	13,240	3,460
Legal and General	7,160	2,250
Commercial Union	5,860	666
Standard Life	5,680	971
Norwich Union	4,900	1,410
Post Office Pension Fund	4,750	1,310
Royal	4,710	571
Eagle Star	3,510	450
National Coal Board Pension Fund	3,370	1,170
Sun Alliance	3,120	754
Guardian Royal Exchange	3,100	611
Electricity Supply Industry Pension Fund	2,800	700
General Accident	2,470	485
British Rail Pension Fund	1,927	391

It will be immediately obvious that it is the large insurance companies and the pension funds of the nationalised industries, such as the National Coal Board, British Rail and the Central Electricity Generating Board, which are the major financiers of new development. Not all of the investment is directly related to the service sector, of course, but the fact remains that a very large proportion of the new shops and offices in Britain and abroad have been developed, and are now owned, by financial institutions.

Even this brief insight into the workings of the property industry will illustrate that the process of development of shops and offices is by no means as simple as one might at first think. Decisions to invest are taken in boardrooms of financial institutions in the city of London or on Wall Street in New York, which affect the shape of many city centres and the functions which are present there.

It should also be noted that some retailers are now major developers and financiers in their own right. In Britain, for instance, ASDA is a major company with extensive property interests. The growth of major out-of-town shopping schemes has also seen the emergence of new types of developers, with the retailers themselves being prominent. This is a repetition of the trend first noted in the U.S., where the major department store interests, such as Sears-Roebuck, were those which financed the out-of-town shopping centres.

The planning process

In most countries it is not possible for a developer to erect a building without first obtaining planning permission. Although this is the most obvious form of control, in practice it is only the lowest in a hierarchy of controls and planning measures which can affect the location of the service sector. In broad terms, there are three levels of spatial control: national, regional and local.

At the national level, governments can implement policies which have an effect on the location of the service sector. Governments in all countries in western Europe have been somewhat more active in endeavouring to control the location of manufacturing rather than that of service activity, although several countries, including Britain and France, have offered incentives to companies to locate office jobs in regions which are in need of economic stimulus. National governments have also been active in controlling some service activities, of which a notable example is out-of-town shopping developments. From 1972 in England and Wales, for instance, all planning applications for new free-standing retail developments over 25,000 sq. ft. (2,328m²) had to be referred to central government for a decision. Essentially this was an effort by central government to impose controls on a form of retailing which it was thought would endanger the existing centres of cities. More recently, in France, the central government has passed legislation designed to control the continued development of out-of-town shopping, following similar measures in West Germany (see Chapter 3).

Planners have also played a part in locating service activities at the regional and sub-regional level. In Britain, the most powerful level of planning is via the *structure plans* which are drawn up by planning authorities for major sub-regions. Structure plans lay down broad policy guidelines for all aspects of the environment and it is these policies which guide planning at the local level. In France, the nearest equivalent of the British structure plan is the *Schéma Directeur d'Aménagement Urbain*, commonly known as the SDAU. The *Schéma Directeur d'Aménagement Urbain de la Région Parisienne* is one example of an SDAU which has attempted to direct the location of service activity. One major problem in the region when the plan was first published in 1965 was an east-west imbalance, since office jobs were predominantly to be found in the west of Paris, whilst the east had relatively few. This distribution was a reflection of the traditional social structure of the city and its wider region, since the more affluent middle class have always lived in the west of the city, while the east has been much more associated with lower socio-economic groups and industry. The regional planners, both in the original plan and in its revision in 1969, 1975 and 1980 have attempted to encourage the development of offices in the east of the region. Similarly, from 1975 until 1985, there was a regional policy to restrict the total amount of new office space to 900,000m² per year. Of this total, 30% was allocated to the new towns, which were a product of the SDAU Plan, as shown in Figure 11. In practice the new towns did not receive as high a

Figure 11 Schéma Directeur d'Aménagement Urbain (SDAU) for Paris Region, 1975

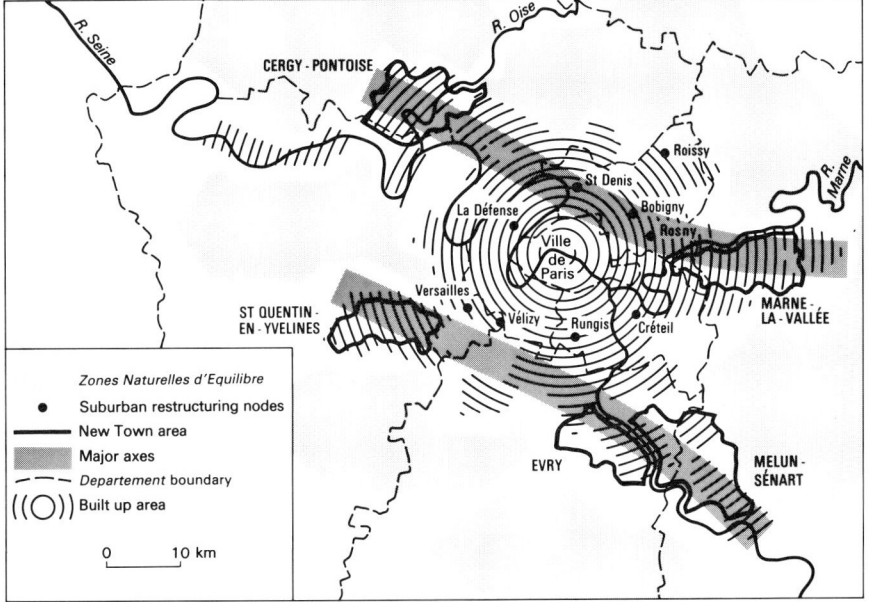

proportion as that intended, but it was a clearly identified attempt to direct office development at a regional level, which operated until January 1985, when controls on office development in the region were eased very considerably.

At the local level, planning permission must be obtained from a local planning authority before any new building can be constructed. In Britain this usually means the district local authority, rather than the county. For example in London, permission would have to be granted by the relevant London borough, whilst in a shire county, such as Berkshire or Cornwall, it would have to be given by the local district or city council. Planning permission generally will only be given if the proposed building conforms to the provisions of a local plan for the area, which will reflect the broader strategies of the structure plan. Continuing the comparison with France, the equivalent plan in that country is the *Plan d'Occupation du Sol*—usually abbreviated to POS—which is produced for each of the lowest tier administrative authorities, the *communes*.

Mention should be made at this point of the enterprise zones which have been designated in various British cities since 1982. In many ways they represent an alternative to active planning polices since only very minimal planning controls operate within them. The rationale behind the setting up of enterprise zones in Britain was to lift many of the restrictions which were felt to be hampering the physical and economic regeneration of areas in serious economic decline, especially in the inner city. Amongst these restrictions, it was felt, were planning regulations, so with only a few exceptions, developers are able to build in enterprise zones without the need to seek formal planning permission. This has already had an effect on some enterprise zones where large scale development involving service industries has already taken place. For instance, the development of an ASDA superstore in the Isle of Dogs in the docklands of east London did not require the planning permission which similar stores required outside the zone, whilst in Gateshead the development of a major retail complex, the Metro Centre, is within the enterprise zone. On an even more extensive scale, there are a number of major retailing developments in the Swansea Enterprise Zone—a process which began in 1983 with the opening of a Tesco superstore. The Llansamlet district of the enterprise zone has since become an important district shopping area (Bromley and Morgan, 1985).

The planning process in Britain has one further provision which has often proved to be very important, especially in large scale developments in the service sector. This is the developer's right to appeal to central government, in the form of the Department of the Environment, in the event of a local authority refusing planning permission. If the development is a particularly large one, or one which is environmentally sensitive, then the Secretary of State for the Environment may set up a public enquiry to examine the application in detail prior to coming to a decision.

Summary

The location of service activity is the result of a series of decisions, many of which are out of the control of the eventual occupier of the shop or office. The dominant role of the financial institutions in developing new shops and offices in Britain is extremely important. Given the scale of investment required for major redevelopment schemes in cities, it seems unlikely to diminish. On the other hand, there is a form of control on location of shops and offices which is imposed through the planning system. It is the interplay of the decisions by investor, developer, planner and occupant which will determine the final pattern of service activities in the city.

Assignments

1 Make a list of the major factors which seem to govern the location of services in the city. For each item give a specific example.
2 Examine Figure 9. Selecting a suitable interval, draw a histogram to show the proportions of the major shopping centres found at varying distances from the centre of Chicago.

Questions from A level examination papers

3 What factors govern the zoning of functions within cities? In what ways have these factors changed in recent years? (University of Cambridge, June 1984)
4 Discuss the use of the bid-rent theory in the study of functions within urban areas. (University of London, June 1986)
5 Identify and explain the main ways in which the provision of shops and offices WITHIN city centres has changed over the last 20 years. (Oxford and Cambridge, June 1983)

3 Retailing change in Europe

An important function of any city is the retailing of goods and services. Retailing, however, is a very varied activity, which includes all manner of outlets from the local corner shop to the department store. In a general sense, there has been an increase in the scale of both retailing companies and individual shops in the last few decades, which has been accompanied by the decline of the independent retailer. Just as important has been the shift in the location of large shops. No longer is the city centre the only location of major shops in the city, since the decentralisation trend which first appeared in North America in the 1950s is now firmly established in Europe, taking retailing to the edge of the built-up area of the city, or even beyond into the open countryside.

Structural differences in European retailing

There are distinct differences in the structure of the retail trade in the various countries of western Europe, with Britain and West Germany being at one end of the spectrum with an important and increasing dominance of their retailing trade by major chain stores. As Table 4 shows, a significant proportion of the retail trade of some countries is carried on through co-operative stores, as well as voluntary groups, such as Mace or Spar. In only three—Switzerland, West Germany and Britain—is more than 10% accounted for by department and variety stores (e.g. Woolworth and Marks and Spencer) or mail order operators. Independent retailers still have over half of the trade in a few countries, notably those in southern Europe such as Spain and Portugal. Elsewhere, their share is declining.

Some care has to be taken in interpreting the data presented in Table 4. For instance, in some countries, the department stores are operated by the co-operative organisations, which decreases the share assigned to 'department and variety stores'. On the

Table 4   Retail trade by organisation in selected European countries (percentages)

	Year	COOP	DVMO	MULT	AFFI	INDT
Britain	1984	5	18	47	5	25
Other EEC						
Belgium	1983	*	7	15	9	69
Denmark	1984	16	*	28	← 56 →	
France	1983	3	8	25	16	48
Ireland	1984	1	8	34	7	50
Netherlands	1985	*	2	27	34	37
Portugal	1984	4	← 40 →		4	52
Spain	1984	3	5	10	8	74
West Germany	1984	3	19	40	26	12
Other non-EEC						
Austria	1984	9	5	22	19	45
Norway	1984	12	← 60 →			28
Sweden	1984	18	3	16	← 63 →	
Switzerland	1985	27	10	13	7	43

Comparable data for other EEC countries not available
* Negligible market share

Key: COOP = Co-operatives
DVMO = Department and Variety Stores, Mail Order Operators
MULT = Multiples, including hypermarket chains
AFFI = Voluntary chains and buying groups
INDT = Non-affiliated, independent retailers

other hand, the broad differences do emerge clearly. There is a marked contrast between those countries where the share of trade carried on in shops owned and operated by independent retailers is declining in the face of a growing dominance of chain stores, and those where the traditional family shop operation is still important.

The decline in the number of retail outlets

There has been a significant decline in the number of retail outlets in western Europe over the whole of the post-war period. In the recent past, this trend has continued unabated. In Britain, for example, in the period from 1971 to 1984, there was a decline of 28% in the number of shops, falling from 471,369 to 342,022. This has been accompanied by an increase in the scale of retail outlets, offering more floor space which is generally owned and operated by major chain store groups.

The increase in private car ownership has encouraged this trend by permitting people to reach large stores more readily, thus to some extent supplanting the need for local facilities. In Britain in 1961, there were 116 private cars per thousand population, a figure which had risen to 280 by 1980, although it is significant that at the time of the 1981 Census, 40% of households in England and Wales did not have the use of a car. For most people, however, small local facilities are no longer needed for the major weekly food shopping since large stores offering significant savings in costs are within easy reach by car. The trend has also been encouraged by the advent of freezers, which allow bulk purchases to be made, and by the wish of consumers to shop once a week or less, rather than buy food on a daily basis. There are, however, two trends to be noted which run counter to these developments. First, new style convenience stores have grown up to offer the possibility of buying goods to top up the major weekly shopping or to serve those people who do not have the use of a private car. Secondly, some major stores, notably Marks and Spencer, have food halls which do provide for people to shop for food more frequently than once per week. Both of these types of retailing, however, can be seen as substitutes for the traditional style of corner shop or local food shopping, which has been in rapid decline.

In many countries, including Britain, the major chain stores have been growing in importance at the expense of the independent sector. Large stores can quite simply make scale economies, ensuring that goods can be offered more cheaply than at the independent shops. They can make and pass on savings to their customers by buying goods in bulk from wholesalers or more commonly, placing orders directly with manufacturers. Once the chain stores were able to introduce such economies of scale, then they began to gain the upper hand in the competition for sites in the city. This has been most obviously illustrated by the retail clothing trade. Twenty years ago, the small independent women's dress shop or men's tailors' shop were commonplace sights, but the introduction of the chain store, offering cheaper mass produced goods as a result of increased scale of operation, very soon brought about the decline of the independent store. A similar trend has affected the food trade, although in some countries admittedly, the small independent food retailer has been able to survive—the French *boulangerie*, *patisserie* and *charcuterie* are good examples. Almost everywhere in Europe, however, large scale food retailing has had an important role to play. In Britain in the food sector the result was that the number of small independent grocery stores fell from 86,505 in 1971 to 47,334 by 1981. Competition from major chain stores obviously was a major cause of this, although physical clearance of some of the inner areas of cities, and with it the traditional corner shop, was also a contributory factor.

Traditional French retailing—a *patisserie*.

It is important to note, however, that the fall in the number of shops cannot be equated simply with the decline of the independent retailer. In Britain during the period 1971–81, the total number of food outlets fell by 46%, with at least 49,000 fewer shops in 1981 than there had been 10 years earlier. But there was a major fall in the number of shops operated by multiple retailers from 10,973 in 1971 to 4,789 in 1981. In 1980 alone, the number of co-operative grocery stores fell by 7.5% from 5,315 to 4,919, whilst outlets owned by multiple grocery retailers fell by 9.6% to just below 5,000. What has happened is that major companies have reduced the number of sales outlets, whilst at the same time increasing the total selling space which they control. For instance, Tesco plc, the food retailing company operating in Britain, now have half the number of stores which they had 20 years ago, but their average size of store has increased considerably, as shown in Figure 12.

The replacement of small outlets by a reduced number of larger ones obviously has very important implications for the location of grocery retailing, since the only sites available for very large retailing units have usually been either towards the edge of the city, or on vacated land in the inner city. Retailers have preferred to move to the edge of the city where the higher income groups live and where car access is far better than in the city centre. In contrast, the inner city has been much less attractive to retailers. There are a number of reasons for this, including the high level of insurance costs, the poor quality of the environment and the fact that their higher income customers are located further away in the outer suburbs.

The rationalisation of retailing—high street mergers

A major reason for the growth of the market share of chain stores is the economies of replication or mass production which are possible in such large organisations. In turn this has led to the formation of larger scale organisations seeking to make such economies. Retailing has therefore become more extensive in scale, encouraged by the increasing number of mergers of major retailing companies. In Britain, for instance, many previously independent high street stores are now part of major retail groups, even though they may retain their original trading name. One British example shows how this trend has recently affected the links between familiar shopping names.

In November 1985, a new retailing group, Storehouse, was formed between Habitat/Mothercare and British Home Stores, to create a company with nearly 900 stores and 30,000 employees. The new company has the advantages of both scale and diversity. In the area of furnishing, it now includes Habitat, Heal's and Conran, whilst in the clothing field, it incorporates Mothercare, Richard Shops and Now. In addition, the group has a half share in Savacentres superstores, which themselves were formed in an attempt by two major retailers, British Home Stores and Sainsbury, to enter into large scale superstore operations from a diversified base.

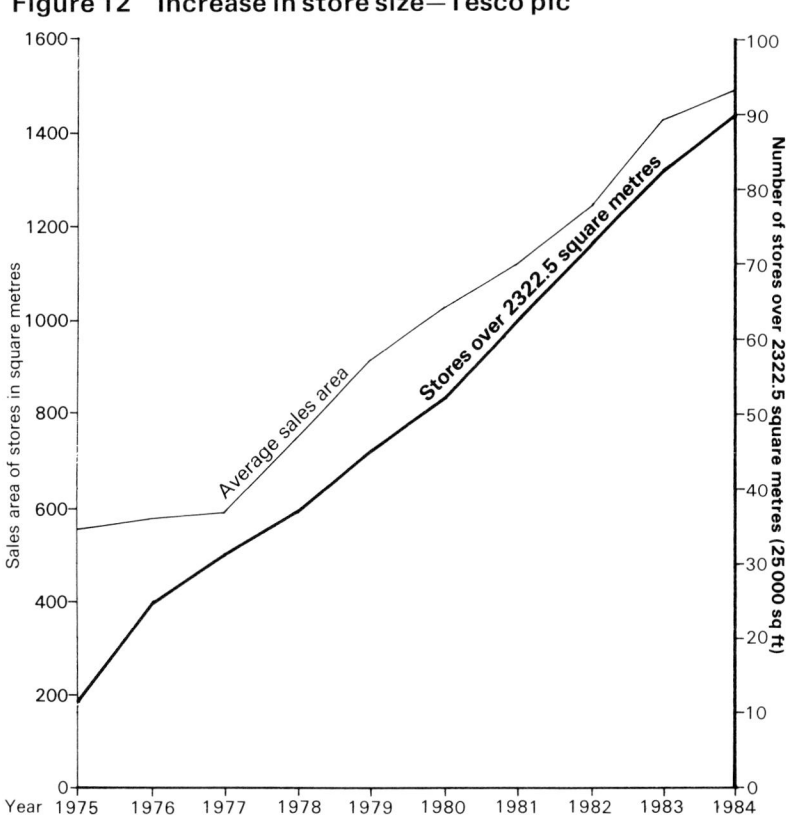

Figure 12 Increase in store size—Tesco plc

A further trend which has taken place is the establishment of shop outlets within larger stores. This 'shop in a shop' concept has two advantages: it enables some traders to enjoy positions of high accessibility without having to incur large capital investment in their own premises and also some large department stores have been willing to lease part of their space in order to increase profitability—an approach which has seen the introduction of Halifax Building Society offices within Debenhams department stores in the last five years.

The internationalisation of retailing—the new European traders

Besides its increasing scale of operation, retailing has also become an international activity. From the point of view of city centres in Europe, this means that some companies are now equally familiar in the shopping centres of France and Germany as they are in Britain. The companies involved in international operations of this type are often British in origin, but this is not always the case. C & A Modes, for instance, is a Dutch company, whilst Benetton is of Italian origin. The growth of fast-food chains, many of which are North American, such as McDonald's and Pizza Hut, has also brought a range of shops to European cities which can now be seen in almost every country.

French retailers have been particularly active in extending their trade overseas, including North and South America—the establishment of a Carrefour hypermarket in Brazil is but one example. Meanwhile, Marks and Spencer, as one of the largest of Britain's stores, has extended its operations overseas, not only to Europe, but also elsewhere and notably to Canada, where it trades from 200 stores. Other British companies, such as Habitat, Mothercare, Etam and the Burton Group have located in France in cities such as Paris and Lyon. Figure 13 shows the location of the overseas outlets of some of these major British companies.

Figure 13 The European shops of three British retailers outside Britain

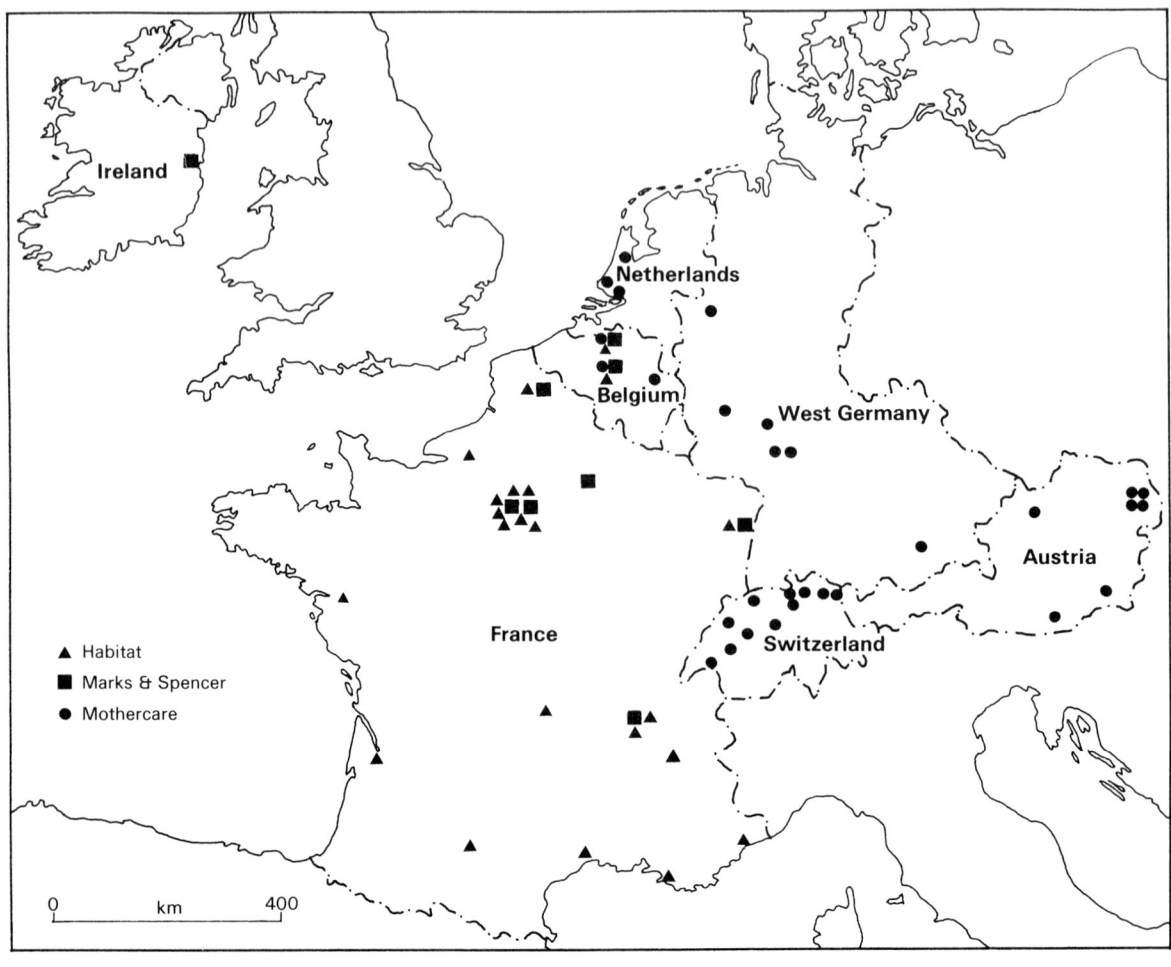

From supermarkets to hypermarkets

It is food retailing particularly which has been transformed by the trends towards an increased scale of establishment, starting with the introduction of the supermarket in the 1950s, leading successively to the superstore and the hypermarket. At the same time, some companies have been especially successful by continuing to trade from smaller units, selling goods at large discounts, with low overhead costs, examples being the Centres E. Leclerc in France and the Albert Heijn shops in West Germany.

At this point it is worth noting that it is Edouard Leclerc who has been credited with preparing the way for large scale food retailing in France (see Ardagh, 1982, 397–400). Starting in 1949 by selling biscuits at a discount in Landerneau, in western Brittany, he moved on to bulk selling of other groceries, but always with the aim of selling with very low profit margins. He was the first to challenge an informal, but illegal pricing system in France whereby prices were fixed by the food industry. Retailers who cut their prices were simply not supplied with further goods to sell. His challenge was successful and now there are over 350 separately owned Centres E. Leclerc. They actually vary in size and in ownership, but they continue to trade in a similar fashion, with low profit margins and little attention to décor and other shop facilities. Once Leclerc had opened the way for large scale food retailing by challenging the pricing system, other companies were able to follow.

The trend towards larger establishments also encouraged locational change to take place, with a general locational shift towards the edge of the city. Although supermarkets, superstores and hypermarkets all conjure up images of large scale retailing, there are important differences between them. More recently, other new types of shops have been introduced to add to the variety of stores now present in European cities. Considering this array of new stores, it is worth examining the characteristics of each, although one difficulty in presenting definitions of each retailing type is that they have been changed over time. The following sections, however, give a broad impression of the characteristics of each type of store and the major differences between them.

Supermarkets

Supermarkets are commonly defined as self-service shops, concentrating on the selling of food, with at least 4,000 sq. ft. (372m²) of selling area floor space. Shops smaller than this have been termed superettes or mini-markets, (Davies, 1984, 18). Supermarkets have increased in size in recent years. In Britain in 1969 only 16% of new supermarkets were larger than 10,000 sq. ft. (930m²), whilst by 1980, 62% were larger than 15,000 sq. ft. (1,400m²), (Institute of Grocery Distribution, 1981, quoted in Davies, 1984). While it is true that the annual rate of growth of supermarkets has declined as new types of retailing have been introduced in the recent past, the number of supermarkets has still risen impressively over the last two decades. In 1961, there were only 500 supermarkets in the countries which now make up the EEC, a figure which had risen to 1,800 by 1971 and over 18,000 by 1980, (Davies, 1984, 56). Their market share has been increasing as they have diversified into general retailing from merely food sales.

Superstores and hypermarkets

In Britain it has become common to make a distinction between superstores and hypermarkets, the latter being somewhat larger and free-standing (as opposed to being part of an existing centre). Elsewhere in Europe, the distinction is less relevant simply because most of the developments have been free-standing stores outside established centres. In terms of their general characteristics, however, there are aspects of their operation which they have in common.

They have a sales area of at least 2,500m², which is on one level. The provision of car-parking is important, with a general ratio of 15 places for every 100m² of selling space. The customer pays for all goods selected at one checkout. Superstores were originally devoted to the selling of a wide range of goods, with at least 35% of the sales being non-food items. More recently, superstores have come to be much more specialised with food based units, DIY units, those specialising in furnishings, electrical goods, and even toys. Opening hours of the stores are extended in the evenings and at weekends, and they frequently open their doors for trading rather later in the mornings than other stores. Other retailing and services are frequently associated with these large stores, including petrol stations, tyre service bays and garden centres, while within the main building other retailing is often present, ranging from bars and cafeterias to chemists and pet shops.

In Britain, the distinction between supermarkets and hypermarkets is partly based on the size of the store, but also on its location and relationship to other shopping facilities. Superstores take over in the size range from supermarkets, having a selling area of 25,000 to 50,000 sq. ft. (2,323–4,647m²). Their emphasis is on food and household goods, with some cheaper lines of electrical goods and clothing. An important feature of a superstore is that it is usually integrated into an existing shopping centre. In

ASDA Superstore.

Britain, good examples of superstores are provided by ASDA, a company which has generally concentrated on developing stores within existing centres.

Hypermarkets are larger than either supermarkets or superstores, with a size range between 50,000 and 100,000 sq. ft. (4,647–9,294m²). In Europe they first appeared in France and Germany, their introduction into Britain being relatively slow, since their location and development was controlled by central government from the early 1970s. They also differ from superstores in that they are usually found outside existing centres, frequently at the edge of the built-up area. The other major difference is that these stores offer a mixed range of goods, including food, clothing, electrical and household goods, with some even having garden centres and car accessory centres.

European hypermarket.

The distinction between a superstore and a hypermarket is one which is most appropriate to Britain, where the two types of stores have been developed. In other countries of the EEC the difference between the two is less clear and most of the large scale new retailing units are termed hypermarkets.

Finally in this general introduction to superstores and hypermarkets, it should be noted that in Britain, there are exceptions to some of these general rules. For instance, some superstores have been developed outside major centres. One example is the development of sites by ASDA, the supermarket chain in association with football clubs, such as Aston Villa AFC in Birmingham, where a new superstore has been built associated with general ground developments. Conversely, hypermarkets have not always been developed on the edge of towns, an example being provided by the Carrefour hypermarket in the centre of Telford New Town.

The varying pace of change towards decentralised retailing

The first hypermarket in France was opened in 1963 at St Geneviève des Bois, on the outskirts of Paris. This marked the beginning of a rapid growth in France, taking the total to 339 by the end of 1976 and 460 by 1981 (defined as food stores over 2,500m²). By that time every major French town had at least one hypermarket and it was not uncommon for cities to have several, strategically placed on the major arterial routes out of the city. In Europe as a whole, however, there have been marked differences in the extent to which hypermarkets had been introduced by the beginning of the 1980s as Table 5 shows.

The importance of hypermarkets to the retail trade as a whole is very clear in the case of West Germany, France and Belgium. In fact, it was in these three countries that hypermarkets were first introduced to Europe, with comparatively few controls on their development. Elsewhere, and later in these countries, governments have been rather more cautious in their

Table 5 Estimates of the number, sales space and market penetration of hypermarkets in selected EEC countries in 1980

	Number	Sales Space '000m²	m² per '000 Population	% of total Retail Trade
Belgium	80	695	70.5	8.9
Denmark	11	128	25.0	3.0
France	455	2,473	46.4	10.8
Italy	16	108	1.9	<1.0
Netherlands	39	181	12.9	2.1
Spain	32	214	5.8	1.0
U.K.	275	1,040	18.7	3.9
West Germany	821	4,950	80.6	10.0

acceptance of this new style of shopping. Nonetheless, by 1984, it was estimated that superstores and hypermarkets accounted for more than 5% of the total retail trade in at least six European countries, including the EEC countries of Britain, France, West Germany, Belgium and Denmark. Only in Italy did the share of trade carried on in hypermarkets and superstores remain at a level of less than 1%.

There have been two main reasons for the reluctance of some governments to welcome this form of shopping without reservation. First, there has been a fear that decentralised facilities would adversely affect the trade of existing centres. Secondly, a concern has been felt that lower income groups, and especially people dependent on public transport, will become increasingly isolated from the major retailing facilities. These misgivings have led to a number of measures specifically designed to restrict the growth of hypermarkets and superstores.

Planning controls on hypermarkets and superstores

In the case of England and Wales, central government issued a Development Control Policy Note to all local planning authorities in 1972, advising them to treat all new developments outside existing centres with caution. In addition, the Department of the Environment, the central government ministry concerned with planning, asked that it should be informed about all proposals for developments of more than 50,000 sq. ft. (4,600m²), (20,000 sq. ft. (1,850m²) in Scotland, where different regulations operated), so that such applications could be 'called in' if necessary, for a decision to be taken by central government. These thresholds were later raised to 100,000 sq. ft. (9,300m²) (in England and Wales in 1976 and in Scotland in 1978). In effect, this put a degree of central control on large scale retailing developments throughout the 1970s. In the period between 1972 and 1976, for instance, 28 proposals in England and Wales were called in for inspection by the Department of the Environment. Of these, only six were granted permission, one was allowed to proceed subject to certain conditions and the rest were rejected, (Davies, 1984, 76–78). On the other hand, many applications were not called in by central government, and were allowed to proceed by local planning authorities.

Since the end of the 1970s and notably since the election of a Conservative government in 1979, policies towards such retailing have been somewhat less restrictive and more new superstores and hypermarkets have been developed.

On the other hand there has been a distinct regional variation in the willingness of planning authorities to permit large scale developments. This is especially well illustrated in the case of superstores, which were developed at a much earlier stage in the north of England than in the south. This may well be attributable to the lack of suitable sites in the south, where the Green Belts have been tightly controlled and there have been few abandoned industrial sites compared to the many such sites available in industrial towns in the north and Midlands. The case of ASDA is a good example to illustrate this regional variation.

The company started its retailing operations in the 1960s and early 1970s, using derelict mill sites in Yorkshire, before moving on to purpose-built premises elsewhere in northern England and the Midlands. Expansion in the south was much more difficult and came only after something of a struggle with local planning authorities, as illustrated by Figure 14.

In the case of France the expansion of hypermarkets was at first encouraged by central government. A response to the major housing shortage in the country in the post-war period had been the construction of very large housing estates, or 'grands ensembles', at the edge of cities. Whilst these housing projects assisted one housing problem, they created others simply because there were insufficient services provided in them. The hypermarkets were therefore seen as one way to fill the gaps in the service provision of the expanding suburbs. Not surprisingly, however, the small shopkeepers were opposed to this major expansion of competing facilities and this culminated in 1972 in the passing of the *Loi Royer* (a law named after the then Minister of Commerce, M. Jean Royer). This new legislation was very wide ranging over many aspects of general business, but provided for control by local committees over all new retailing which exceeded 1,500m², (1,000m² in the case of small towns with populations less than 40,000). Since that time, although hypermarkets have been developed, there have been fewer new ones opened each year than previously and the emphasis has been on the building of smaller stores—supermarkets and superettes. This change has been in part due to the legislation, but is also the result of changes in the French economy, including economic recession, since the height of the hypermarket expansion period.

In West Germany, controls were imposed at the local level, but once again, rather late in the day to prevent these major stores affecting existing centres. The government in Italy, like that in Britain, has also acted to restrict the number of superstores. This debate as to how far new retailing development has an adverse impact on neighbouring shopping centres has been a lively one in Europe during the last 20

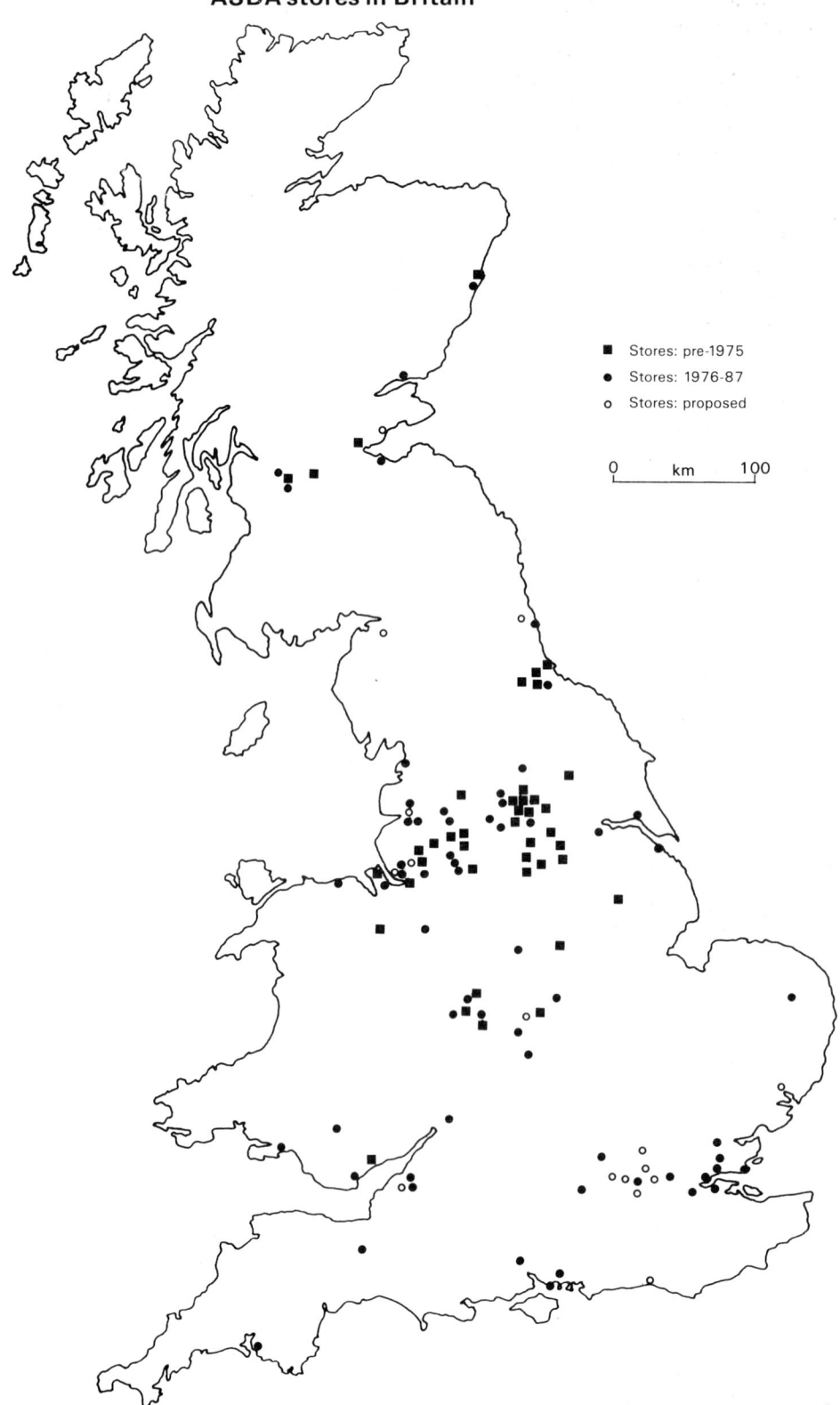

Figure 14 The phases of development and distribution of ASDA stores in Britain

■ Stores: pre-1975
● Stores: 1976-87
○ Stores: proposed

years and has affected all the planning decisions associated with retailing, including both hypermarkets and even larger retailing developments. The decline of the city centres and the growth of out of town retailing which has taken place in the U.S. has been seen as a pattern which must not be repeated in Europe. It is the British government, however, which has been the most reluctant to allow these developments to take place.

Convenience stores

Before examining developments even larger in scale than hypermarkets, it is worth pausing to consider one response to the large scale food retailing which has transformed many cities. Whilst major companies have been moving outwards, new stores have been established in traditional locations. These stores are known as convenience stores and were first developed in North America, where the 7-Eleven chain has been particularly successful. They remain open late at night—even 24 hours in some instances—and offer a local service for 'topping up' food and other purchases. In addition, they provide a very valuable service to those less mobile members of society who cannot reach the large new stores on the edge of the city.

Convenience store.

The trend towards this kind of store has become well established in Britain during the 1980s, with the major oil companies also beginning to move into convenience retailing by setting up stores in association with their petrol stations. By 1985, it was estimated that there were about 750 such convenience stores in Britain, the majority being part of the Spar grocery group, which converted 650 Spar grocers shops to 'Eight Till Late' convenience stores (*Financial Times*, 19 January 1985). In Britain where 40% of packaged grocery goods are now sold from fewer than 800 outlets, owned by Tesco, ASDA, Sainsbury and others, there is a well established need for a small local store to supply food and other items which are needed because supplies have run out or they have been forgotten on the major shopping trip.

Other large-scale shopping developments

Retail warehouses

A relatively recent innovation has been the introduction of retail warehouses. These are usually housed in purpose-built premises at the edge of the city, although originally they were in former industrial or storage buildings. They usually specialise in one area of retailing, such as DIY, electrical goods or furniture. Whereas in France for well over 10 years, the retailing of furnishing has been decentralised to stores located on major radial routes leading from the city, in Britain, this form of shopping has been the product of the 1980s. Essentially, the principles which underlie these stores are the same as those which have led to new types of food shops, with large car-parking facilities, late opening hours, and shopping provided on a single level, although in many cases these stores also have a very large area given over to warehousing.

IKEA store at Evry, south of Paris.

An example of the retail warehouse concept developed to its maximum is the IKEA furniture store at Evry, a new town south of Paris. It occupies a six hectare site and has a floor area of 21,000m². Of that, approximately 10,000m² is actual selling space and 7,000m² is warehousing. Generally customers view the goods in the display area, then order their furniture at a sales desk, picking up their goods, which are normally 'flat-packed', from the warehouse. Car-parking is provided for 850 customers' cars. The store is open from 11 a.m. each day, including Sunday, with extended opening hours in the evening on a number of days of the week.

Regional shopping centres

The largest of the new retailing developments is the regional shopping centre. This type of centre was first developed in North America and consists of a covered shopping precinct or mall, with two or three major stores, usually acting as so-called *anchor stores*. The anchor stores are seen as the major generators of pedestrian traffic and their location often at either end of a mall therefore promotes a through-flow of pedestrians within the centre. The shopping malls themselves are often on at least two levels and contain, in the largest centres, as many as 200 shops, specialising in shopping (or comparison) goods as opposed to convenience goods. Essentially, the regional shopping centre took shopping facilities which had previously been in the city centre out to a more accessible suburban site. In many North American cities that was all too often literally the case and the city centre was left bereft of its major shopping facilities. Department stores and major clothing stores moved out to a purpose-built mall, surrounded by car-parking facilities to serve the suburban shopper. The sites which were developed were commonly at the intersection of freeways outside the city, since these were the new points of peak accessibility, as discussed in the previous chapter.

European reaction to this particular retailing innovation has been mixed. In Britain, the general policy has been to resist such large scale out-of-town developments and concentrate instead on the redevelopment of existing centres. There are a number of reasons for this general reluctance to move towards suburban dominated shopping patterns. First, there is no doubt that evidence from the U.S. has been examined carefully by planners and politicians. There, in very many cities, suburban shopping centres have virtually stripped the downtown area of its major retailing, leading to a major need to revitalise the city centre. Inevitably, there has been a feeling that Britain's cities should not suffer in that way.

Secondly, there are many vested interests in the existing city centre, including retailers and financial institutions, who would be loath to see their capital investment undermined by a move from the centre. It is interesting to note that until 1984 one of Britain's leading retailers, Marks and Spencer, had no plans for major out-of-town stores and remained firmly in support of the city centre. Since then, however, the company has introduced a new policy into its development programme and as a result, its largest store to date was opened in 1986 at the Metro Centre in Gateshead. Future plans include other stores in suburban locations, such as Broxbourne near Cheshunt in Hertfordshire in 1988 and Handforth, near Wilmslow, Cheshire in 1991.

A further argument against large scale shopping located at out-of-town or peripheral sites has been that some people are not sufficiently mobile to have access to such sites, although some companies have already tackled that problem by providing free bus services to hypermarkets and superstores located at the edge of town. There is also a strong conservation argument against the further erosion of agricultural or recreational land at the edge of the city. In some cases, this is an even stronger argument when a possible encroachment into a designated Green Belt is involved. This general opposition has meant that at least until the very recent past, there has only been one major regional shopping centre in Britain outside established city centres and that was located in North London at Brent Cross, where a centre of over 90,000m², was opened in 1976.

Meanwhile, major redevelopment has taken place to provide regional centres in the central areas of many major European cities. British examples are the Arndale Centre in Manchester, the Eldon Square Centre in Newcastle-upon-Tyne and the Victoria Centre in Nottingham. Many of these in-town centres have adopted the same design concept as the out-of-town regional centre, with a covered mall and a complex of shops with one or two major stores, the anchor stores, linked by a wide variety of shopping goods stores.

In several French cities, alternative city centre facilities have been provided at sites close to, but separated from the centre in order to provide an alternative commercial focus of both shops and offices. For instance, in Lyon, La Part Dieu was built on a former barracks site since the traditional centre, the Presqu'île, formed by the narrow spit of land between the River Saône and the River Rhône, was not capable of expansion for offices or retailing, (Tuppen, 1977) (see also a fuller description in Chapter 4). In Bordeaux, the Mériadeck Centre was built to provide a new commercial and office centre. On a smaller scale in Rouen, the Saint Sever quarter, a kilometre from the city centre, was transformed to include a new shopping centre and associated hotels and offices to try to form a second pole of attraction away from the city centre. The real success of these policies in providing high quality regional shopping centre facilities can be questioned, but they do offer an alternative both to the massive redevelopment of an existing centre, which may not be possible in a city where urban conservation policies are in operation, and to the abandonment of the city centre itself for its suburbs.

The European city which has seen the fullest development of North American style retailing in suburban locations is Paris. Starting in 1969 with the opening of a regional shopping centre near Versailles, a comprehensive network of such centres has been built, as shown in Figure 15.

Figure 15 Regional shopping centres in Paris region

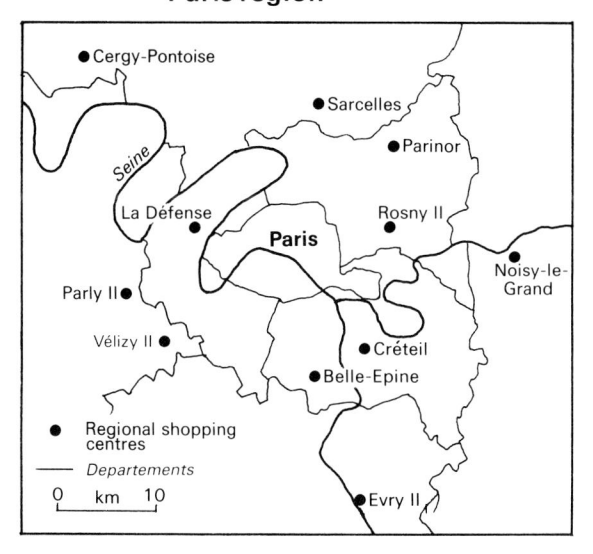

The first centre, Parly II, was relatively small with a gross floor area of 55,000m², and 3,000 parking places, well situated close to the *autoroute* (motorway), running westwards out of Paris. The name of the centre was chosen originally because of its close similarity to Paris Deux—reflecting the wishes and ambition of the developer to duplicate the facilities of Paris in the suburbs. The shopping centre followed the established pattern with two anchor stores, and approximately 100 other shops, a garden centre and an autocentre. Parly II was followed by the development of other centres, including Belle-Epine (68,000m²) and Vélizy II (88,000m²). A number of the new regional centres were built as part of the new towns being developed in the Paris region during the 1970s, following the regional plan for the city originally published in 1965. Three of the five new towns which were eventually built—Evry, Cergy-Pontoise and Marne-la-Vallée—had new regional shopping centres, although that at Marne-la-Vallée was somewhat smaller than the other two.

One centre at Créteil, in the south-eastern suburbs of the city illustrates the main characteristics of this type of centre. Créteil itself was developed not as a new town but as a suburban growth pole in the regional plan. Créteil-Soleil, its regional shopping centre, has a floor area of 78,000m², of which 27,800m² was originally devoted to department and variety stores. There are a further 190 shops and car parking for 3,000 cars (see Figure 16). The centre is unusual in

Figure 16 Plan of Créteil Soleil Regional Shopping Centre in south-east Paris

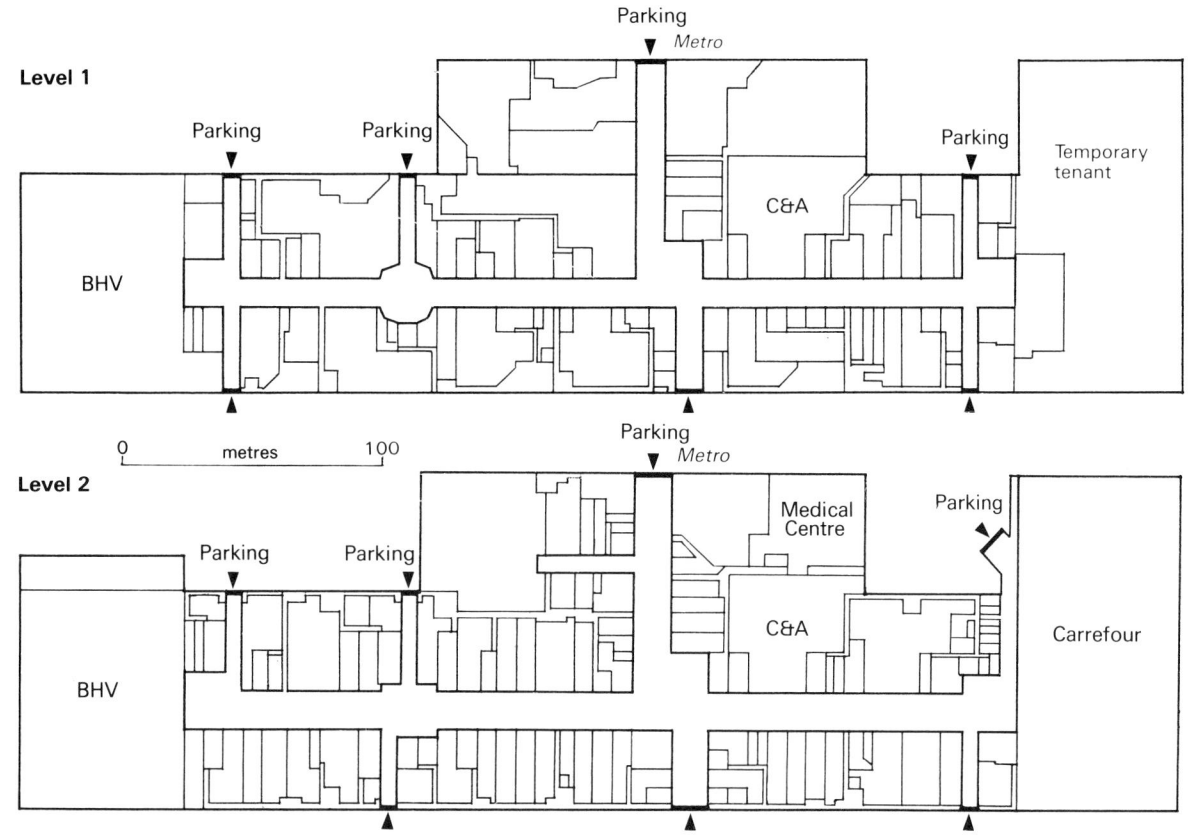

that it has direct access to a *metro* station, as well as being on bus routes, which give it a better accessibility for non-car owners than that offered by many similar centres.

The rapid expansion of regional shopping centres did lead to some problems, which are best illustrated by Créteil-Soleil. In 1977, one store group, which includes Printemps, a major French department store, needed to make financial savings on a large scale. It sought to effect this by cutting back on its out-of-town operations, suggesting that it had overstretched its resources somewhat by developing stores in the major regional shopping centres. The result was that Printemps withdrew from Créteil-Soleil, leaving the urgent need to replace it with a store which could act as a major generator of pedestrian flows. In the event, most of the remaining space was taken over by Carrefour, the French hypermarket chain, but this type of shopping in a major regional shopping centre of this style is not seen as the ideal.

Brent Cross—a regional shopping centre in Britain

The nearest British equivalent to a North American regional shopping centre is Brent Cross, a centre of 90,000m². This development in north-west London is not strictly an out-of-town centre, since it is actually located well within the suburbs, having been built on land which was not intensively used, but which enjoyed extremely good accessibility. Its location at the junction of the North Circular Road and the M1 motorway meant that 1.25 million people lived within 20–25 minutes driving time of the centre (Newby and Shepherd, 1979).

Brent Cross—interior view.

Construction of the centre began in 1970 and it opened for trading six years later. Its success was immediate and caused major problems of local accessibility. The original car-parking provision of 3,500 spaces had to be enlarged by a further 1,000 spaces in a multi-storey development. One difference between this centre and its North American counterparts is that, like Créteil-Soleil, it is well served by public transport. In this case, bus services run into the centre's own bus station, from which there is direct access to the shops.

The design of Brent Cross follows a common pattern with two major department stores, John Lewis and Fenwick, acting as anchor stores at either end of a shopping mall, which contains 90 standard sized shops, in addition to four large multiple stores—C & A, Marks and Spencer, Boots and W. H. Smith. 85% of its sales are in shopping goods, although there is also a Waitrose supermarket within the centre.

Eastgate Centre, Basildon—the extension of an existing centre

The trend to reinforce major centres rather than building major out-of-town centres has already been mentioned, but there are also signs in Britain that some major shopping centres are being located in intermediate locations, which are neither out-of-town nor in major regional cities. They are being developed in medium sized towns, with the intention of serving a much wider area than the town itself. One example is the Eastgate centre which opened in 1986 in Basildon, in Essex.

Eastgate Centre, Basildon.

Basildon itself was designated as one of Britain's first new towns in 1949 and grew to a population of 100,000. Crucially, with the development of the road network and the rise in car ownership, by 1986, approximately one million people lived within 30 minutes' driving time, as shown in Figure 17. The development of a large regional shopping centre was seen as an expansion of the existing facilities of the new town.

Basildon town centre was originally focused on Town Square (see Figure 18a), with some major multiple stores trading in the town. Phase 1 (24,500m²) of the new development was an extension to the town centre and included a Savacentre store with associated par-parking, as shown in Figure 18b.

Central Basildon—aerial view.

Figure 17 Basildon—regional location and 30 minute driving time zone, as seen by the developers of the Eastgate Centre

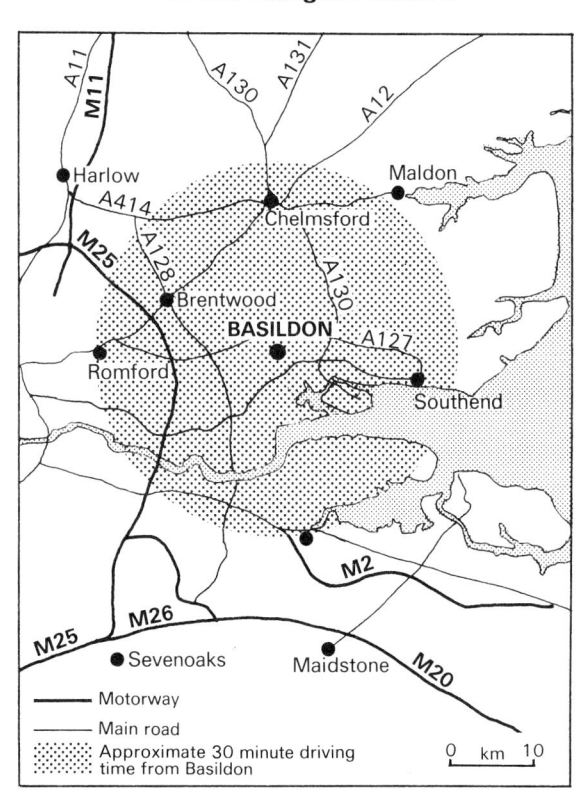

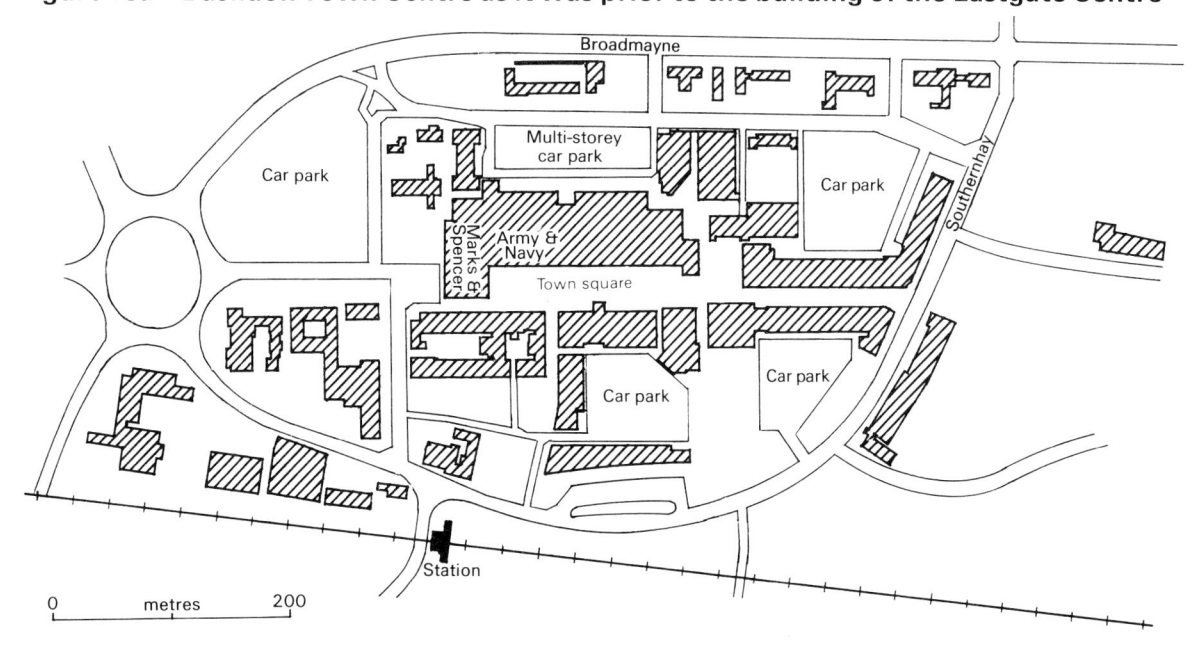

Figure 18a Basildon Town Centre as it was prior to the building of the Eastgate Centre

Figure 18b Basildon Town Centre, with the addition of the Eastgate Centre

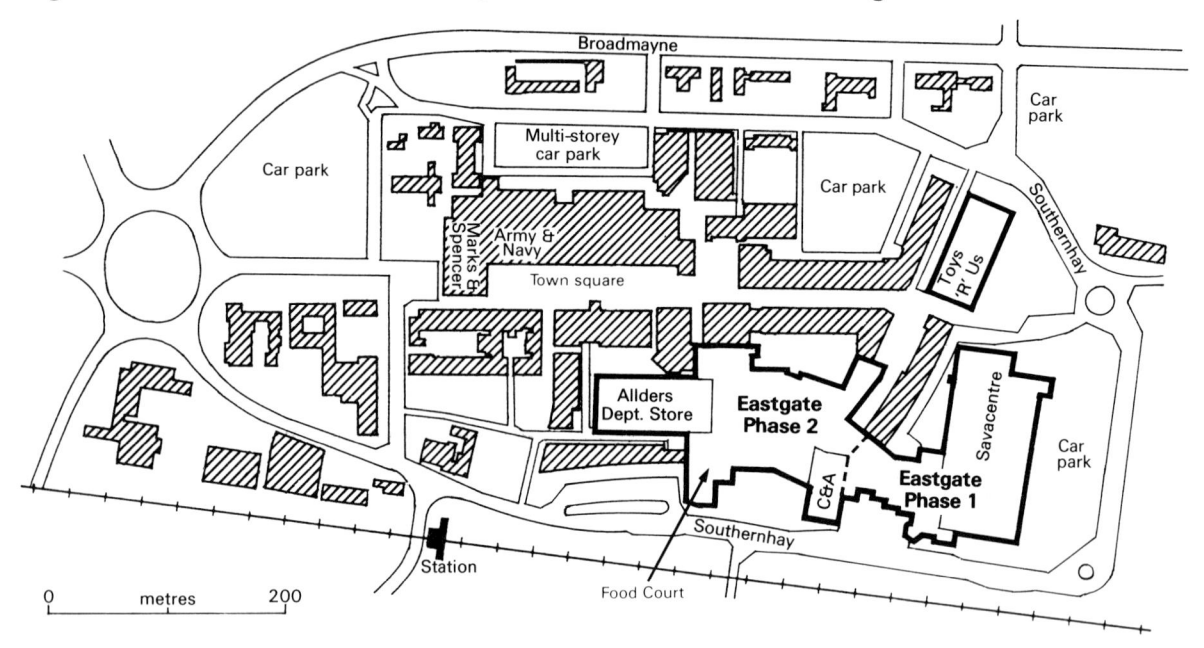

Figure 19 Cross-sectional plan of Eastgate Centre

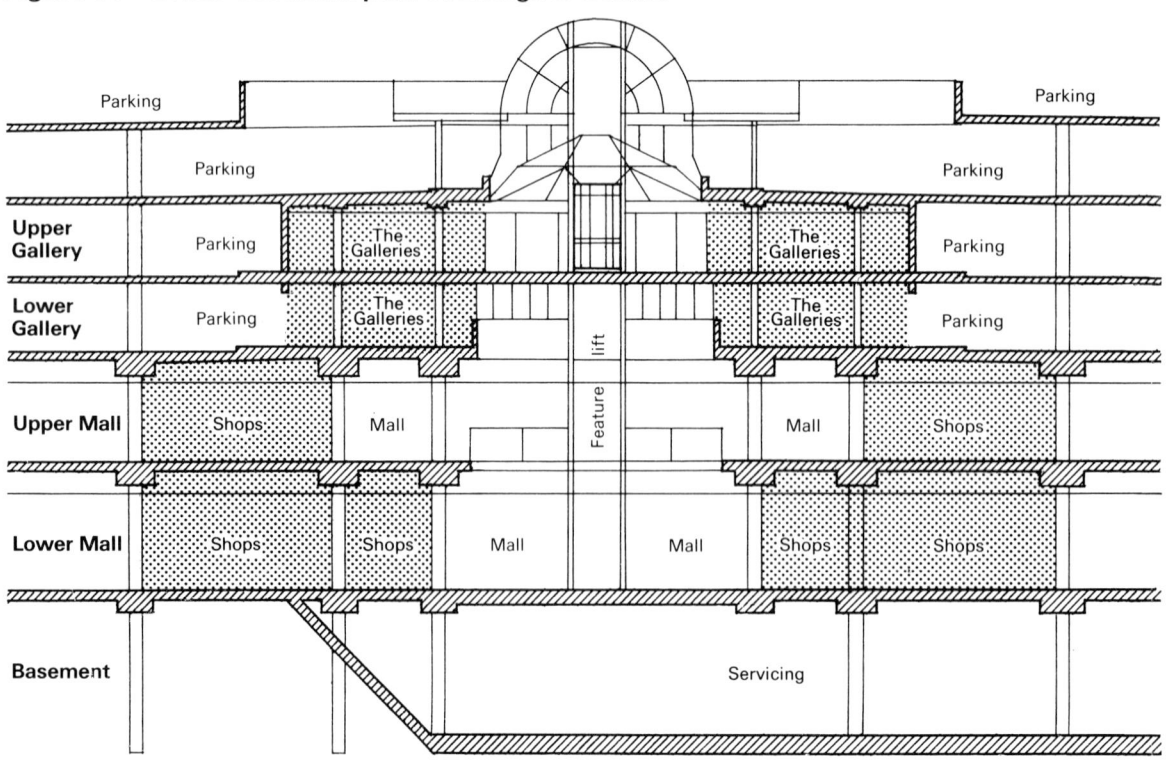

Phase 2 (43,500m²) of the centre was built on a 2.73 hectare site (see Figure 18b), which was previously two surface car parks, entailing the loss of 500 car-parking spaces. These had to be replaced in the new development, and the outline planning brief was for a major department store of up to 18,500m², with a similar amount of retail space in individual units, 9,200m² of offices and parking for 1,000 cars.

Figure 20 Impact of Eldon Square Centre on central Newcastle-upon-Tyne

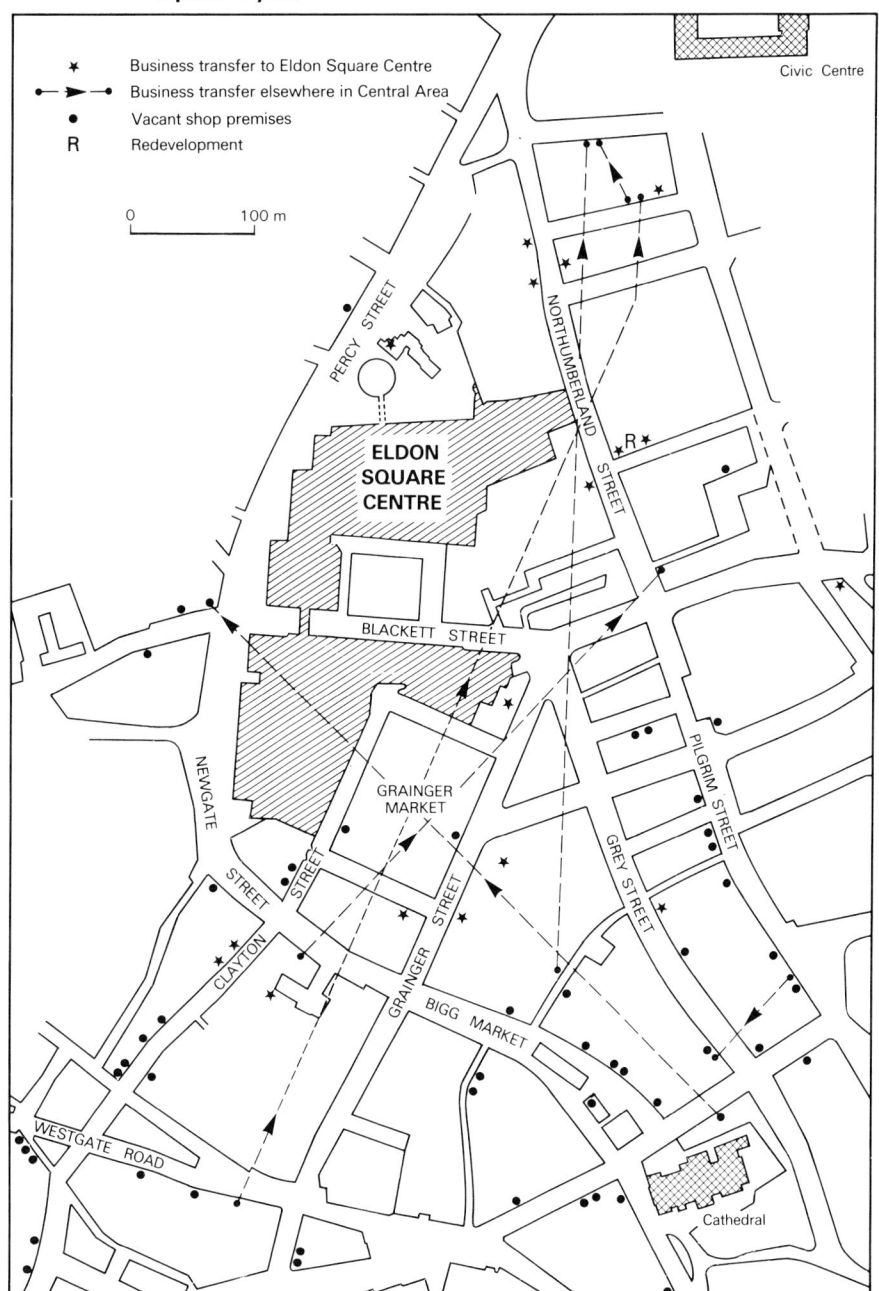

The department store, Allders, became the second anchor store, counterbalancing Savacentre from Phase 1, as shown in Figure 18b. The site for the centre was a restricted one and produced problems associated with servicing the shops and providing car parking. In the event, car parks were provided at and above the second floor of the new development, whilst servicing was provided in part from basement access, illustrated in Figure 19.

One feature of the centre which is now increasingly common in covered shopping centres is the Food Court, offering a range of food to be taken away or consumed on the premises. In this case, there are eight food kiosks, with a seating area for 200 people. Besides the major retail units on the lower two levels, there are smaller shop units on the upper storey, called the Galleries, where 42 individual shops have been let to a wide variety of relatively small traders, including jewellers, card and gift shops, and exclusive fashion shops.

The development of the Eastgate centre in Basildon illustrates the care which has to be exercised to produce a new shopping centre which is properly integrated, as opposed to one which is merely a new centre grafted on to older, outdated shops.

There are currently a number of planning applications being considered for major new centres within British cities, but as the discussion of Basildon indicates, development of major regional centres within existing towns and cities is a difficult task. One problem is that while attractive new shopping precincts may draw in customers, it may be at the expense of the rest of the centre. In 1976, the opening of the 69,500m² Eldon Square centre in Newcastle-upon-Tyne, for instance, made a dramatic impact on the shopping patterns of the city centre, capturing one third of the trade of the city centre in its first year of operating, and causing some shifts in the location of stores within the central area of the city (see Figure 20). The building of a new centre may cause some shops to seek new sites to be closer to the major retailing outlets within the centre, especially if new transport facilities are included in the development. This may lead to a chain reaction as other stores move, leading to a decrease in the pedestrian traffic in the original locations, forcing other stores to consider their position and either move themselves or to go out of business.

Summary

In this chapter, a wide range of new shopping forms has been discussed within the general context of a decline in the absolute number of shops, counterbalanced by an increase in the scale of shopping facilities. The move towards the edge of town away from the centre is one which has been important, but not as yet universal within the countries of Europe. Other new trends are affecting shopping environments quite dramatically. The rise of new designer shops, such as Next, has been important to British town centres, whilst the trend towards integrating leisure and recreation interests with retailing will certainly mean in the future that a trip to the shops is far more than a routine chore.

Assignments

1 Examine Table 5. Examine the strength of the relationship between the percentage of total retail trade and the square metreage/000 population of hypermarket floorspace. Also calculate the average hypermarket floorspace for each of the named countries. To what extent is there a relationship between this average and the percentage of total retail trade?
2 Compare Table 5 with Table 4. To what extent can it be said that hypermarket penetration in the countries of the EEC is related to the nature of the competition?

Questions from A level examination papers

3 Identify and discuss the main ways in which the trend towards larger-scale operation is affecting the nature and location of tertiary activities. (Oxford and Cambridge, June 1982)
4 Examine, with examples, the view that different urban land-uses have different locational requirements. (London, June 1983)
5 Examine the arguments for and against the construction of out-of-town shopping centres. (London, January 1986)
6 'The location of tertiary activity is determined by accessibility.' Discuss. (London, January 1985)

4
Offices in European cities

The commercial centres of most major cities grew up in the nineteenth century. At that time, administration moved from industrial locations to the more accessible sites of the city centre, close to financiers, brokers, and insurers who were located there, whilst manufacturing remained on its original site. At the same time, the commercial functions of the city were becoming more complex, requiring larger, purpose-built premises. Since that time, city centres have become more and more dominated by office functions and by the buildings which accommodate them. The office has indeed become the symbol of the modern city.

What actually happens in offices? The simple answer is that they are dealing in information—processing it in various ways, transmitting it and making decisions based on it. These functions, of course, employ a very large number of people and until the recent past there has been every sign that the numbers of office workers would continue to grow very rapidly. Two major changes, however, have come to challenge this traditional view of offices and office activity. First, there has been a revolution in what is now termed *information technology*. The routine office work involving the filing away of information, retrieving it when required, extracting items to be used in other documents and all the other mundane tasks, has been transformed by advances in information technology. Both the filing of information and its retrieval can be done via computerised data bases, which can be linked to word processing facilities to incorporate information on file into letters or reports directly. Routine tasks which previously were either very time-consuming, or required a lot of clerical assistance, can now be carried out more quickly and with fewer staff involved. The second process involves the challenge to the traditional concentration of offices which have produced the characteristic high rise skylines of city centres throughout the western world. Concentration also means congestion, high land values, competition for labour and a poor working environment. Not surprisingly, therefore, many companies have begun to examine the advantages of moving to less central locations. It is this locational change which is the principal subject of this chapter.

Centralisation/deconcentration

Until 20 or 30 years ago, there were few signs that offices would be located anywhere other than in city centres. The only exceptions to this were those offices such as solicitors or estate agents which were offering a local service function. There were a number of reasons for this. First, the central location offered accessibility, since it was at the hub of a transport network which focused on the city. Since there was still a very high dependence on public transport for the journey to work, other locations were not accessible to the great majority of the working population of the city. A second reason was that those people employed in offices needed the personal links with other offices located at the centre, so that business could be conducted quickly and efficiently.

Increasingly the question was asked whether offices needed to be at the centre of the city. With modern communications, contact could be maintained easily enough without the face-to-face contact which was seen as being an important attribute of a central location. While the telephone had offered that facility for a long time, it was greatly enhanced by the introduction of more advanced forms of telecommunication, offering innovations such as teleconferencing and the instant transmission of documents from one part of the country to another. Since the majority of contacts made by office workers outside the firm are *programmed*, dealing with routine matters, a central location is hardly important. Studies have shown that only 15–20% of office contacts are *orientation* contacts, involving negotiations or exchanges of information, which might require a 'person to person' meeting (Goddard, 1973).

The continuing importance of face-to-face contact in some areas of commercial activity should not, however, be overlooked. Improvements in communication technology may take time to become well accepted, so that traditional ways of doing business may still survive. In the City of London, where the number of foreign banks grew from 73 in 1960, to 158 in 1970 and 428 by 1982, many of the interbank

Stock Exchange—transactions in progress.

transactions still require personal delivery of documents. Trading on the London exchanges, dealing in stocks and shares and insurance, has traditionally been done almost entirely by personal contact. The deregulation of the London markets, permitting more people to trade in stocks, shares and securities, which took place in October 1986—the so-called Big Bang—was accompanied by the introduction of the computerisation of transactions, eliminating by 1987 personal dealing on the floor of the Stock Exchange.

Office location trends

In Britain, the post–war property boom which followed the reconstruction of many cities continued to provide new offices at the centre. This was true, not only of London and Britain's major provincial cities but of almost all the major commercial centres in Europe. As early as the late 1950s, however, there were some signs that companies were willing to consider other locations, especially if the rising rents of the city centre could be avoided by moving to another less expensive location. In some cities, planners encouraged this move in order to avoid putting intolerable pressure on city centres for the large scale redevelopment of parts of the city, many of which had considerable historical value and required careful conservation measures.

In the case of London, while some decentralisation was taking place, the property boom of the 1950s and 1960s continued to concentrate offices in the city centre. Indeed by 1965, the British government had to introduce controls on the location of offices in London to try to curb the increasing congestion of the centre. These took the form of Office Development Permits (ODPs), which were required for any new office development or major expansion of office space over 3,000 sq. ft. (297m²). The area to which the controls were applied was soon extended to include all the south-east and the Midlands, although by 1970, the latter region and East Anglia had been removed from control. The lower limit for developments requiring an ODP was raised gradually to reach 30,000 sq. ft. (2,788m²) by 1977, but two years later, in 1979, the system of control was abolished completely.

Even without such government intervention, however, a large number of companies chose to relocate at least some of their routine office functions away

IBM (UK) in Portsmouth: the North Harbour office complex.

from the congestion and high rents of central London. Many of them, although by no means all, were assisted by an advisory body which was set up by the government in 1963 to offer information to companies considering a move from the capital. This body was known as the Location of Offices Bureau and existed until early 1980. It had no financial incentives to offer to companies to move, but it could act as a clearing house for information and many companies used its services. Amongst the companies to relocate much of their routine office work from London, and in some cases, the entire company, were Eagle Star Insurance to Cheltenham, National Westminster Bank to Bristol, Zurich Insurance and IBM (UK) to Portsmouth.

By 1977 central government had become concerned about the decline of major cities, including London, so the Location of Offices Bureau was given a different role to play. It was assigned the task of attracting international companies to Britain and encouraging the location of offices in inner urban areas of British cities, which by then were seen to be in sharp economic decline. A similar body has operated in France since 1974, with the same brief as that originally given to LOB. This is the *Association Bureaux-Provinces*, which advises companies wishing to move from Paris with the general aim of developing the tertiary service sector in the provinces.

Emerging patterns of office location

Processes of relocation have produced a very varied pattern of office location, with changes at both the regional and the urban levels. At the regional level, offices have frequently moved away from the major city to smaller centres, or even into greenfield sites away from major settlements, but close to good communications facilities. Rents in the City of London in 1986 were approaching £300 per m², compared, for example, to £145 per m² in Tunbridge Wells, and £116 per m² in St Albans. Outside the south-east, rents were considerably lower, with levels around £70 per m² in the centres of Liverpool, Manchester and Birmingham. This differential in costs of office accommodation has obviously made companies examine their requirements for central London locations very carefully indeed.

At the urban level, a number of different sites have been chosen. These have ranged from locations close or adjacent to the original city centre, where offices have expanded into the inner suburbs, through to more peripheral locations. Some of these are typically close to airports which are themselves a peripheral land use, but which have drawn offices to them because of the increased accessibility which they offer. Other peripheral locations have attracted offices because of the increased accessibility derived from a new motorway network, in much the same way as retailing has been attracted to such locations. Figure 21 illustrates the range of intra-urban office locations which have emerged from these trends.

The essential characteristics of a number of these locations will be examined in more detail, with some detailed case studies of individual projects. It will be clear from this analysis that locational freedom, or at the least locational flexibility, has become a reality for many office users, since there now exists a very considerable range of locations which have attracted office development.

City centre

The city centre still attracts office users. They occupy existing office developments, new developments and premises which have been renovated or refurbished. The refurbishing of offices involves maintaining the structure of the building, including its facade, but completely modernising its interior—usually nowadays with the aim of putting in new communi-

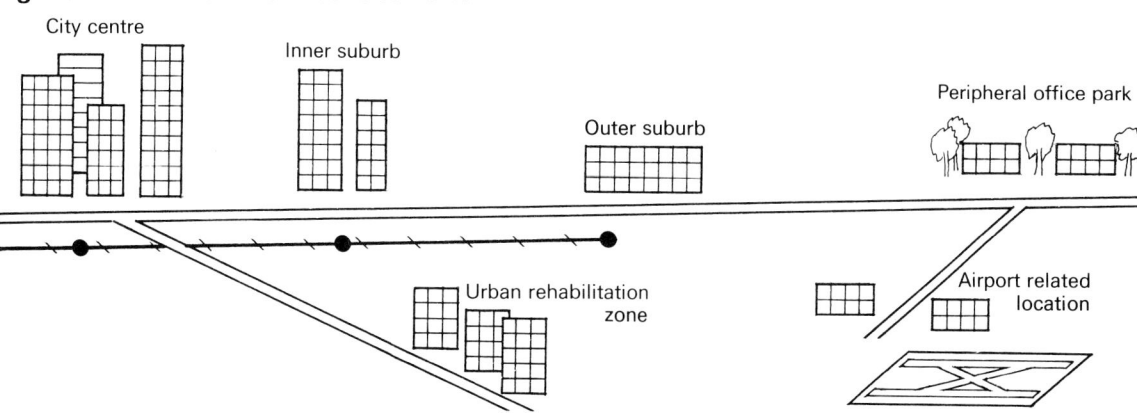

Figure 21 Model of office locations

cations and computer technology which might not have been available in the old premises. In some cities, refurbished offices are very important since planning restrictions may restrict the supply of brand new offices. Elsewhere, however, rents for offices are generally highest at the centre; where planning authorities permit, new developments are still taking place there.

Inner urban office centre

Office centres have often developed as an overflow from the traditional central area. Frequently the process started as a series of conversions of residential property to offices, before major redevelopment took over and a large scale office development has emerged. In Frankfurt in West Germany, the West End district is an early example of this expansion. Between 1961 and 1970, the district lost 22% of its population as offices moved in. This met with some local opposition, but the process continued so that West End now has nearly one fifth of Frankfurt's office space, (Burtenshaw et al., 1981, 72).

Similar opposition has met proposals to develop major office facilities to take overflow from the City of London on the South Bank of the Thames. In that case, the land use being displaced was largely manufacturing or dockside storage facilities rather than residential facilities. The greatest opposition was mounted against a proposal to develop the Coin Street area to provide a very large office scheme, adjacent to the National Theatre and Thames Television on the South Bank. The two local authorities involved, Lambeth and Southwark, and the local community were opposed to the further development of offices on the grounds that office jobs were not needed by the local population, many of whom were unemployed as a result of the rundown of the docks and local waterfront industry. Office jobs would merely attract more workers in from the suburbs and beyond. In the case of Southwark, a survey in 1979 of office workers in offices constructed since 1970 in the borough revealed that only 9% lived locally. It was also estimated that of all the office floor space in Southwark, nearly 1,000,000m² in all, only 2.9% had a local service function. Local opposition was mounted in community newspapers, as well as through the more formal channels of the planning system, as illustrated by the cartoon extracted from the Coin Street News.

The planning process was very protracted. There was a six month public enquiry in 1979, which resulted in no planning permission being granted. A second public enquiry in 1981 resulted in planning permission being given to two schemes—one to the developers, Greycoats Commercial Properties, for their scheme including office development of 82,170m² and the other for a more balanced development of housing, offices and industry which had been proposed by a consortium of local community groups. Eventually in 1984, the property developer withdrew from the scheme, leaving the way for the project favoured by the local community.

Coin Street News.

The inner urban office centre has therefore been controversial in many cities. Whereas such developments may be seen as natural developments from the centre, they do disrupt existing land uses and communities. Twenty years ago there was little effective opposition to such developments, but now there is often strong opposition, based largely on the grounds of the adverse impact on the local community.

Planned office centre

An alternative to the piecemeal expansion of the centre is a completely new office centre or office park. With properly co-ordinated planning, community interests are less likely to be prejudiced and furthermore, it has often been possible to incorporate other uses in such developments to make them more than merely centres of office employment. There are several examples in European cities of this form of office centre, including City-Nord in Hamburg, La Part Dieu in Lyon and La Défense in Paris. The characteristics of each of these developments will be considered here in some detail.

Hamburg City-Nord City-Nord lies six kilometres north of the city centre and represents a deliberate planning policy to create a high quality business environment away from the central area of the city. Work commenced in 1961, when the pressure on inner Hamburg for new office space became too intense (Husain, 1980). Transport congestion and a fear that the skyline of the city would become overwhelmed by skyscraper office blocks persuaded the city authorities of the need to provide an alternative office location. The new development had to be sufficiently attractive to persuade both new companies and those already operating in central Hamburg to locate there.

City-Nord is a large project of 600,000m² of offices, employing some 30,000 people. The aim has been to create a high quality environment, with large areas given over to landscaping. Of the 95 hectare site, some 30% has in fact been designated as landscaped open space. Contact has been maintained with the city centre via underground rail links. It has enjoyed some success in achieving its aim of attracting offices from central Hamburg, including the oil companies, BP and Esso. Eight companies have moved out to City-Nord from the centre of Hamburg, vacating some 100,000m² of offices, allowing other small firms to become established or to expand close to the centre (Husain, 1980, 132).

La Part Dieu—Lyon French cities have often adopted the concept of the brand new office centre as a solution to the growth pressures exerted by the increasing demand for office space. As a general term for these projects, the French have coined the phrase '*centre directionnel*' and they can be found in a number of major cities. The major Paris office centre at La Défense is the largest of these developments and is considered in more detail below. Of those in

La Part Dieu, Lyon.

provincial cities, the largest is La Part Dieu in Lyon, which is a new office and commercial centre created on land formerly occupied by military barracks, (Tuppen, 1977). The site occupies 30 hectares in an inner suburban location, some 1.5 kilometres to the east of the original city centre (see Figure 22).

The need for a new centre for commercial and business premises stemmed partly from the restricted site of the existing central business quarter, and partly from the growth of tertiary activities, which contributed significantly to the 4.4% annual job growth in the city between 1968 and 1975.

The centre has 400,000m² of offices, besides a regional shopping centre of 110,000m², which opened in 1975, a new city library and a large 2,000 seat

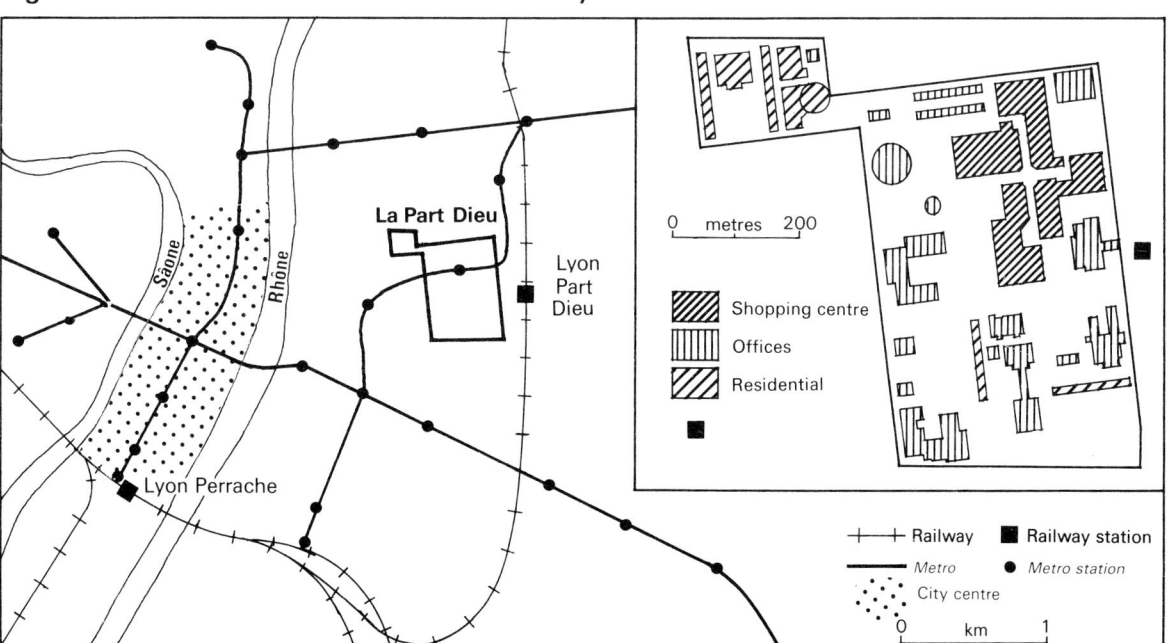

Figure 22 La Part Dieu and its location in Lyon

auditorium (Tuppen, 1977). Of major importance are the new transport facilities which give exceptionally good access to La Part Dieu at both the urban and the national level. As part of the scheme, a new railway station has been built to accommodate the new high speed express train, the TGV (*Train à Grande Vitesse*), linking Lyon to Paris and more recently to the south. This new mainline railway station was necessary to ensure that the city's main central station (Lyon Perrache) did not become over-congested. Besides this mainline railway development, Lyon has developed a completely new underground train (*metro*) system in the last 10 years and La Part Dieu is now well linked to the rest of the city via this new network.

La Défense The final example of a planned office park is La Défense. It lies close to key communication routes (see Figure 23). In the mid-1950s, an exhibition centre was built on a site then occupied by a mixture of of residential and industrial development. The three local authorities concerned, Courbevoie, Nanterre and Puteaux obtained the support of the French government to develop the site further as a major office centre.

In 1958, a development authority (*Etablissement pour l'Aménagement de La Défense*—EPAD) was set up to plan the area and then develop the land. The site was divided into two parts—an eastern sector (Zone A), of 160 hectares. and a second zone (Zone B),

La Défense, Paris.

further away from central Paris, of 600 hectares. The latter has been developed with housing, parkland and some public functions, including a university at Nanterre, while the former has been the principal business sector. The plan for Zone A, the business quarter shown in Figure 24, included 1.55 million m^2 of offices, a major regional shopping centre, and residential development of 7,585 dwellings. When it is completed, it is anticipated that almost 70,000 office workers will be employed at La Défense.

A new complex network of transport facilities also has to be provided, including an express *metro* service (the RER), linking La Défense to Paris, a station on the conventional *metro*, a station for the ordinary train service (SNCF) and a bus station. All of these facilities are now provided below a pedes-

Figure 23   Paris and La Défense

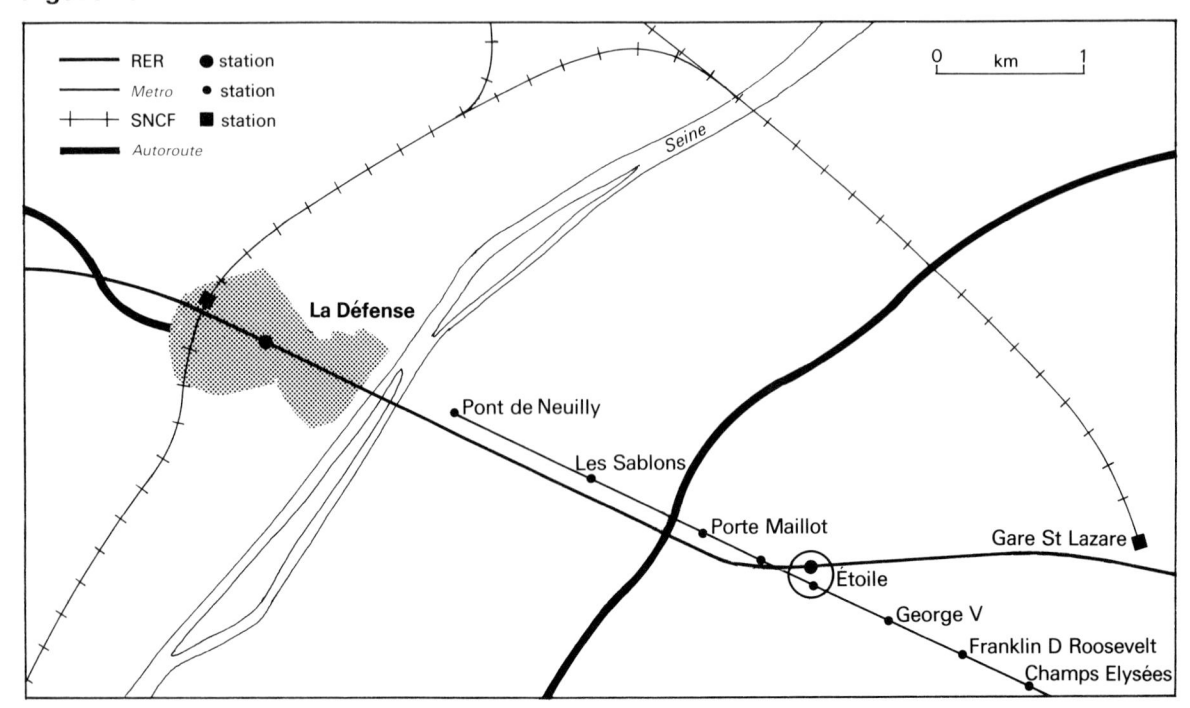

Figure 24 The business quarter (Zone A) of La Défense and phases in its development

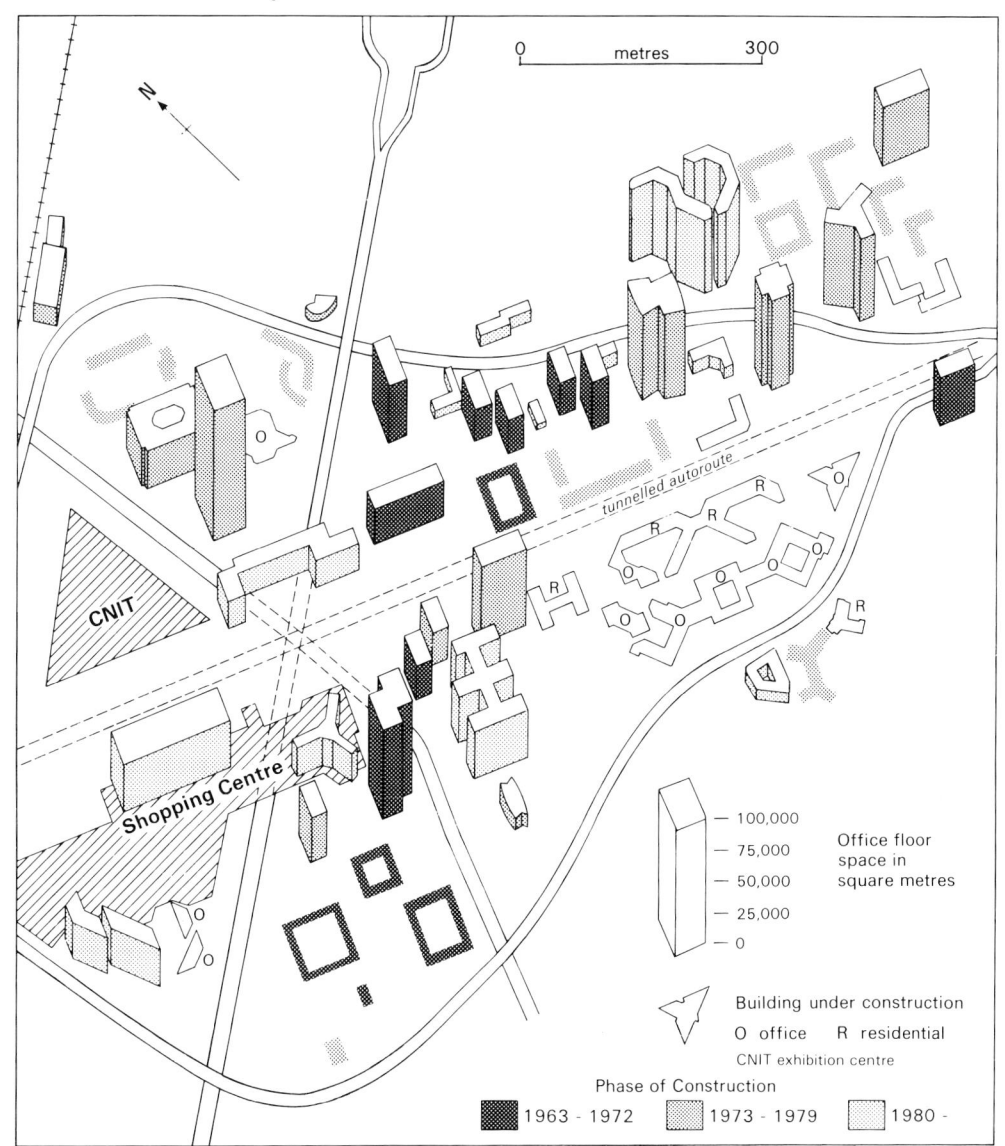

trian deck which covers the whole of the complex. With car parking and hotels added, the project is one of the largest planned business complexes in the world.

The building of La Défense (combined with years of control over building heights) has meant that there are few skyscrapers in the centre of the city and certainly no cluster of tall buildings marking a central business district so characteristic of major North American cities, or even the City of London. Major companies have taken the decision to move to La Défense and today it houses the headquarters of a large number of French companies as well as the French headquarters of many foreign companies. Examples include IBM (France), which occupies 105,000m² of office space, and four oil companies, occupying 186,000m² in total, 126,000m² of which houses Elf-Aquitaine, the major French oil company. Besides these, the major French banks, insurance companies, car manufacturers, chemical companies and many other industrial concerns all have offices at La Défense.

Suburban office centres

In some cities, suburban centres have attracted offices on an extensive scale. The rising cost of city centre

41

office rents has encouraged this development of offices in pre-existing suburban centres, particularly when they are well linked with the city either by public transport, by motorway, or by both. In almost every major city in Europe, offices have now undergone a degree of suburbanisation.

Outer metropolitan growth centres

Whilst suburban offices have become commonplace in most cities, in the major cities of Europe the same process of decentralisation has been evident, but it has operated on a larger scale. As Europe's major cities have grown and congestion of the centre has become more apparent, growth of offices has often been deflected to the edge of the metropolitan area, where small and medium sized towns have then grown very rapidly. The best example in Europe of this process has occurred to the west of London, but in a similar fashion, towns of the Paris basin, such as Chartres and Orléans have experienced the growth of office jobs. In the Netherlands, towns on the fringe of the Randstad, such as Arnhem, have received an overflow of offices from the major centres.

Business parks

Business or office parks have been created in a variety of locations by private enterprise. Business parks were first developed in the U.S., but have now become firmly established in Europe. They consist of low density office accommodation, usually set in landscaped surroundings. Many companies now give a high priority to the standard of the work environment and business parks can offer much more on this score than a city centre site. In addition, business parks are likely to be closer to the place of residence of the workers of a company. Ideally, the site should be very accessible in terms of its proximity to the motorway system and to other forms of transport such as major airports.

Windmill Hill—an example of a business park One of the most vigorously growing areas in Britain in terms of office development is the M4 corridor, stretching westwards along the motorway from London. This zone has seen the development of numerous office parks which are sited outside towns such as Maidenhead, Reading, Swindon and Bristol. Windmill Hill is one example, sited to the west of Swindon. Its location is shown in Figure 25.

The first phase of the Windmill Hill business park comprises four separate office units ranging in size between 8,000 sq. ft. (744m²) and 18,000 sq. ft. (1,673m²), totalling some 50,000 sq. ft. (4,646m²). They are shown in the photograph on page 43, with a plan of the park itself shown in Figure 26. Each unit is a two storey building, each fitted to a very high standard, including air-conditioning, with provision for full computer installations.

Figure 25 Location of Windmill Hill Business Park, Swindon

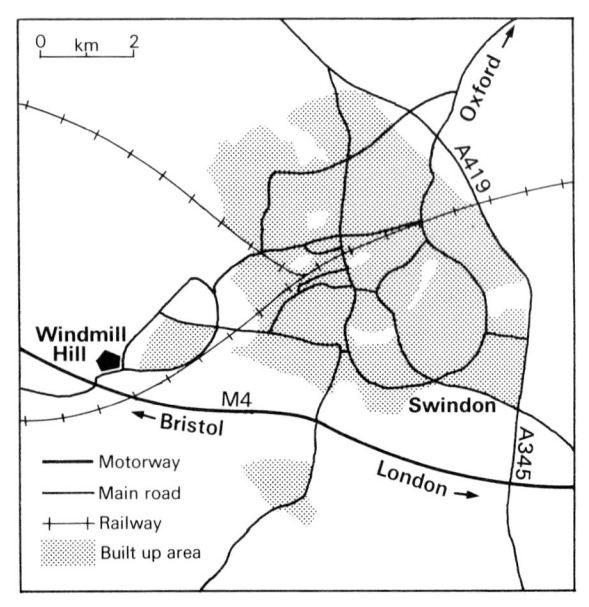

Figure 26 Plan of Windmill Hill Business Park

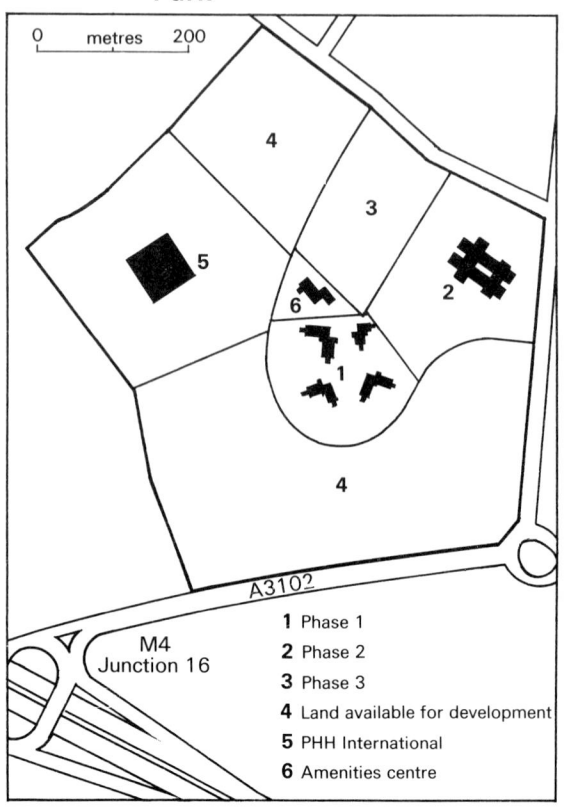

1 Phase 1
2 Phase 2
3 Phase 3
4 Land available for development
5 PHH International
6 Amenities centre

Windmill Hill Business Park, Swindon.

The second phase of the park is a headquarters building of 68,750 sq. ft. (6,389m²), designed to be let to a variety of occupants. A further sector of the park accommodates the European headquarters of PHH International, a major car fleet management company. Clearly, a business park of this type can offer a far higher standard of environment than that of a city centre. What is more, it can offer a very high degree of accessibility, both nationally and internationally, being adjacent to the M4 and within one hour's drive of London's Heathrow Airport. The other advantage of this location for office development is the attraction of the region as a place to live. It is somewhat easier to attract highly skilled or qualified workers to a high quality environment in rural Wiltshire than to the City of London.

Figure 27   Location of Norly 2, Lyon

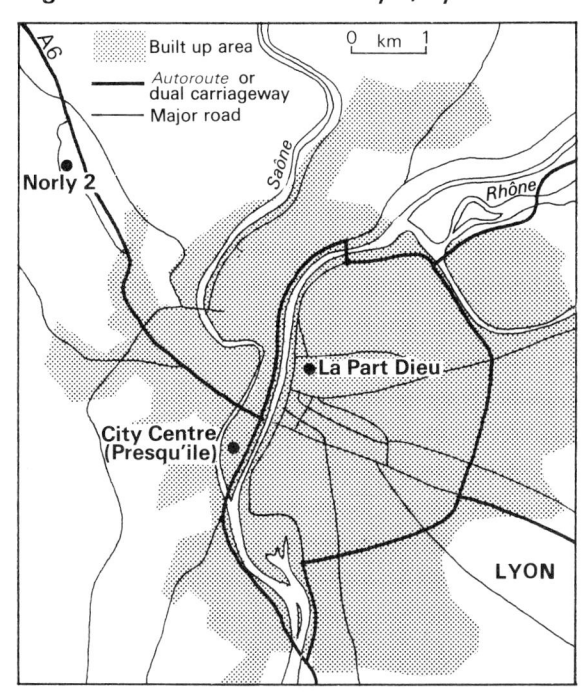

Norly 2—Lyon   Business parks have been developed elsewhere in Europe. In France a smaller example than those considered above has been developed to the north-west of Lyon. The park is called Norly 2 and it illustrates particularly well the locating characteristics which are typical of such developments, lying just off the main *autoroute* (A6) on the northern approach to the city (see Figure 27). It has a total of 2,600m² of office space, in three linked buildings, set in landscaped grounds and surrounded by over 130 car parking places. This particular development has the added advantage of being served by public transport.

Redeveloped inner urban zone

Increasingly, city authorities are faced with the problem of dereliction of the inner city. The decline of manufacturing has been such that large areas of the city have been left vacant, creating a major planning problem. In the case of London's Docklands, a partial solution was the designation of a part of the former docks, the Isle of Dogs, as an enterprise zone. Within this area, planning regulations are relaxed, and there are financial attractions for developers and occupiers, such as rate-free periods. The area has attracted a wide variety of functions, including some industry, a new superstore, which has already been noted above

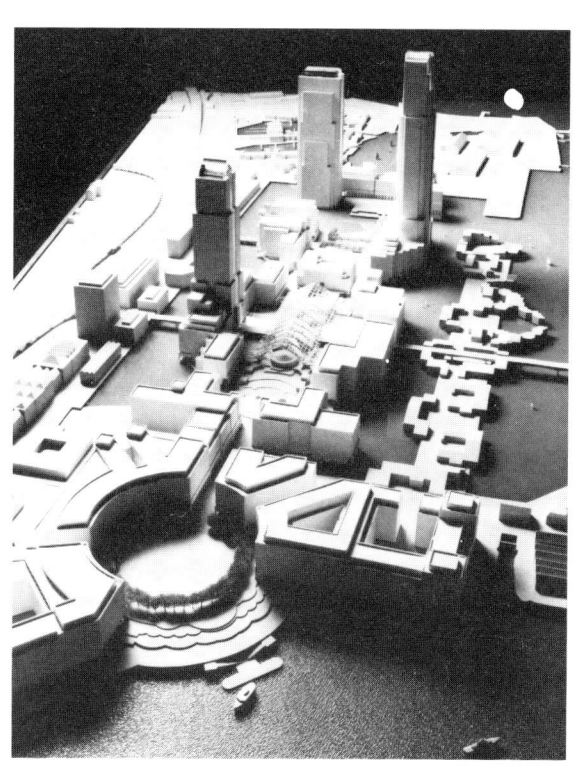

Office development proposals for Canary Wharf, Isle of Dogs.

(see page 18) and most significantly perhaps, offices. An office centre which is planned for the Isle of Dogs will be one of the largest developments of its kind in the world.

The scheme is planned for Canary Wharf and envisages the building of 12 million sq. ft. (1.12 million m²) of offices, which will eventually employ between 40,000 and 45,000 people. In space terms, this is an approximate equivalent of constructing 24 office blocks each the size of the existing NatWest tower—the tallest building in the City of London. The demand for this vast office space comes from the growth of financial services within the City of London. In part this stems from the deregulation of the Stock Exchange, but in other major centres, such as New York, the growth of employment in this sector has recently been as high as 21–22% per annum. The developers, an American consortium, feel that this level of demand will justify this immense scale of development.

Canary Wharf is linked to the city by the new Docklands Light Railway, which will be extended further into the City of London, to join the existing underground system at Bank (see Figure 28). The development has not been universally welcomed, largely because of its vast scale, but even if it is eventually modified, it still stands as an example of the way in which office development can now be seriously considered outside established centres.

Other developments are already taking place in the Isle of Dogs, such as the 1.5 million sq. ft. (139,400m²) Heron Quays project, which includes offices and apartments, and South Quay Plaza, which consists of 400,000 sq. ft. (37,174m²) of new offices.

All these developments raise important questions relating to the local environment and community. In the case of London Docklands, the local communities such as the Isle of Dogs were tightly knit with successive generations working in the docks or associated industries. The almost complete decline of the docks in the Port of London has left many people unemployed. The local community wished to see manufacturing jobs created, employing local skills, but the new jobs already planned and created are frequently 'white collar' office jobs. In an area like Docklands, as the job profile changes, so does the residential mix. New homes for higher income groups are being built and old warehouses are being converted into luxury apartments. House prices rise to a level which can be met by those employed in office jobs, not those in manual work, setting up tensions in the local community. In social terms then there are obvious disadvantages to large scale office development in areas which previously housed other functions.

Summary

Although offices are still to be found in the centre of

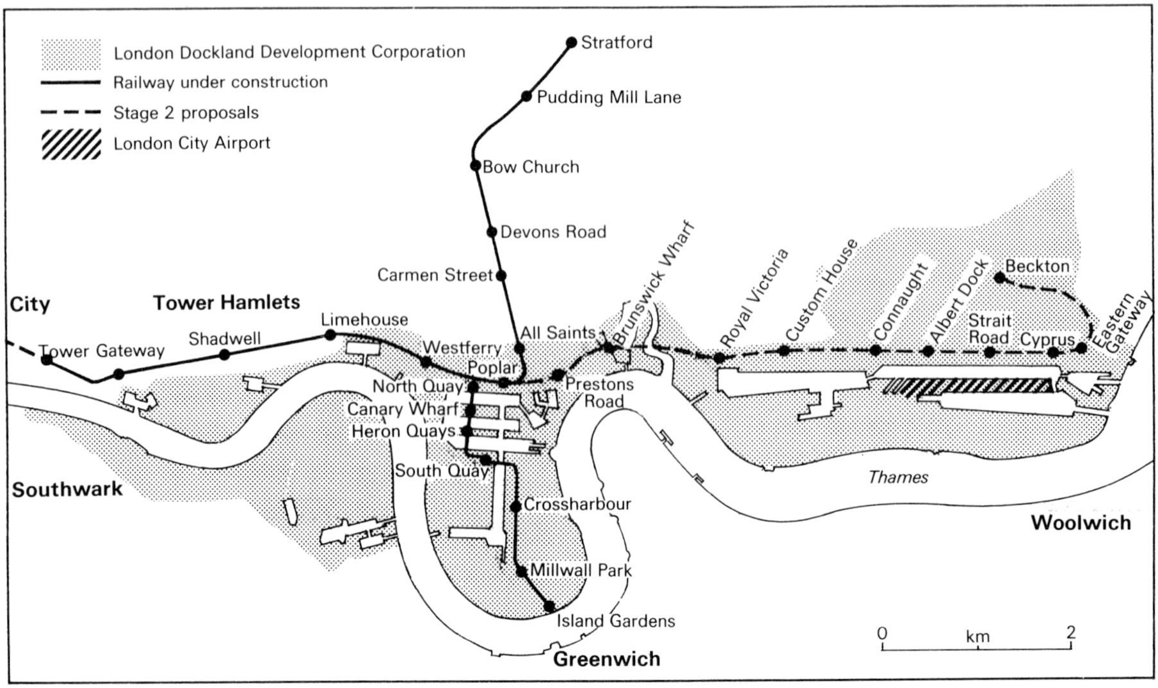

Figure 28 The Docklands Light Railway, London City Airport and Canary Wharf

cities in western Europe, there are now a wide variety of locations from which office users can choose. Those who still value the contact environment of the city centre will be located there, together with others who have remained there through processes of inertia and tradition. For others, a move out of town may be rejected because of the problems of the daily journey to work for their employees. Yet throughout Europe, a new pattern of offices is emerging which is more dispersed, reflecting the fact that information—both the raw material and product of offices—can be transmitted almost without regard to physical location. The extent to which the office function itself has been transformed by the new technology which has been so important to this locational freedom is discussed in the following chapter.

Assignments

Questions from A level examination papers

1 (a) Explain why different land-users compete with each other to occupy sites in or near city centres.
(b) For any ONE large city within the EEC (i) describe the clustering of functions which has occurred within the central business district (CBD) and inner city; (ii) account for the development of distinctive specialist functional zones. (Joint Matriculation Board, June 1981)

2 (a) Explain the reasons why certain types of shops and offices are strongly concentrated within the central business districts of towns and cities, whereas other types are more widely distributed.
(b) Discuss the extent to which the detailed land-use distributions in the central business district is related to (i) accessibility to the pedestrian; (ii) proximity to complementary land-uses. (Joint Matriculation Board, June 1982)

3 The larger the city, the more attractive it becomes as a location for offices and commercial services.
(a) Why is this so?
(b) What are the effects of this on the structure of the city? (London, June 1982)

5 The service sector and new technology

Almost all services involve either the handling of information or a financial transaction. In many cases both activities are involved, while in others only one of them takes place. The purchase of a foreign holiday at the local travel agency means that reservations have to be made with tour operators, hotels and airlines, often involving information travelling thousands of miles. The customer has to pay the travel agent, who in turn must pay those providing the travel services which have been booked. One relatively simple act will have involved the exchange of many items of detailed information as well as the completion of a detailed financial transaction and is typical of the millions of such transactions which take place every day.

The way in which these transactions are performed is undergoing a major revolution. No longer need information be stored on a piece of paper, to be sent from one office to another, whether it is the one next door or the one on the other side of the globe. Instead, information in the form of data, or even complete

Figure 29 The development of the pocket calculator, 1957–83

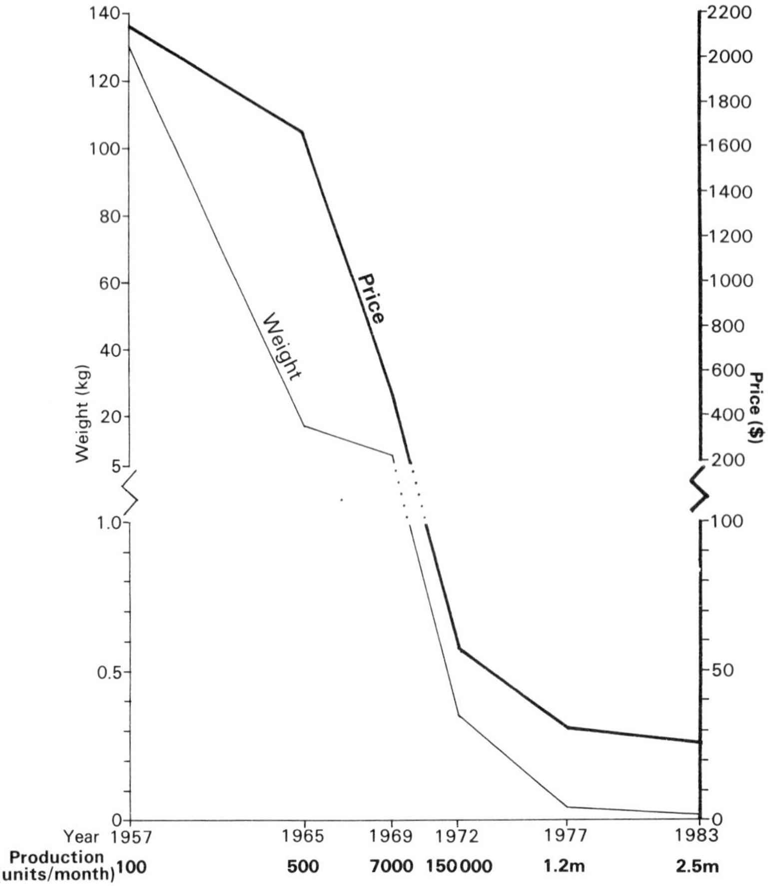

documents can be transmitted worldwide. Customers in shops do not need to hand over cash for their purchases, but can pay instead in a variety of ways. Some of these are well established, like credit card transactions, whilst others use new technology to a much greater extent and transfer funds directly from the customer's bank account to that of the retailer.

In this chapter, some of the new technologies which have been adopted in shops and offices will be discussed, with the aim of assessing how far the location of these services is likely to be affected by such developments. In many cases it may be too early to predict accurately the real effect, but certain trends are appearing which suggest that our traditional view of the location of services may be changed quite fundamentally by the innovation of new technology.

There are some basic questions to be answered. First, what are the new technologies and how do they operate to affect the service industry? Second, what impact will they have on employment and location?

The pace of change

The introduction of new technology is not new; a succession of inventions has changed the way in which the service sector works, although few have previously changed its location. In the office sector, the introduction of technology could be said to have started in earnest in the 1870s, when Remington, the typewriter manufacturer, first started commercial production. By 1900, the company were producing 20,000 machines per year and the office and office work were never to be the same again. More recently, telephones and the telex have been introduced. In the last 100 years there has been a dramatic change in the way in which offices are organised and in the handling and transmission of information. These changes, however, have accelerated rapidly in the last 10 years.

The pace of change can be illustrated by looking at the development of the pocket calculator, as shown in Figure 29. The chart refers to Casio calculators, each carrying out the same basic functions. From 1957 to 1969, the pace of change was certainly very significant, but hardly dramatic. From then, however, the pace of innovation stepped up remarkably, reflecting the introduction of the silicon chip, which has enabled more and more sophisticated machines to be produced in increasing numbers.

The electronic office

Advances in computer technology have created the possibility of a totally electronic office. Essentially it has five elements, which are shown in Figure 30.

The individual office worker has a *work station*, at which he or she receives information in order that it can be processed, or a decision can be made based on it. The work station is linked to other work stations and to a *central processing unit* via a *local area network* (LAN). This means that the office worker

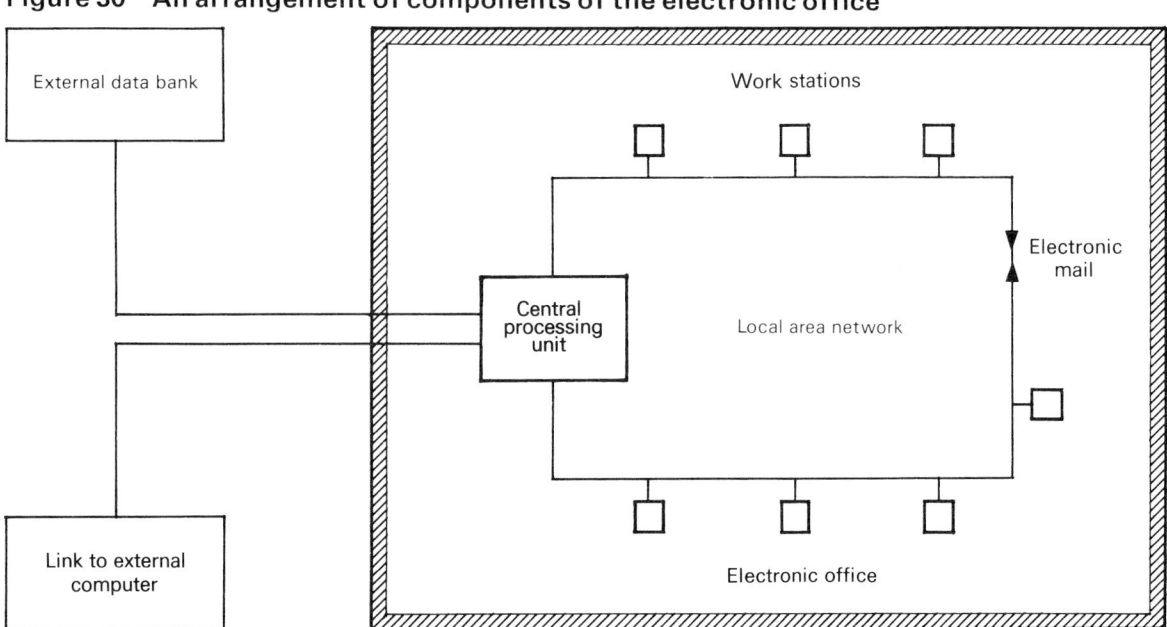

Figure 30   An arrangement of components of the electronic office

can receive information from any other work station, can use the central processor to carry out complex calculations, or possibly to act as a word processor, and can be linked to any other system outside the office. This may mean linking to an *external database*, such as Prestel, or perhaps to another branch of the company located in another part of the country.

Work stations can be very sophisticated and may allow an operator to move documents from one filing 'cabinet' to another using icons or mice, which move an arrow on the screen, transforming an ordinary desk into what could be termed an electronic desktop. Some computer systems have touch-sensitive screens to handle and file information.

LANs are essentially systems for linking together computers, work stations, memories and printers, so that information can be shared rapidly and effectively. An LAN may be likened to a highway along which 'packets' of information are sent on their journey from one point to another.

External data banks are sources of information which can be accessed from an office. The general term for these external facilities is 'videotex' systems (known in Britain as 'viewdata'), perhaps the best known being Prestel. Some data banks contain information which is useful to all businesses, relating for instance to financial information on exchange rates or share prices. Others are more specialised and serve one particular service or industry.

The extent to which any one office has been transformed into an electronic office will of course vary quite widely. Word processors are now commonplace, but LANs and the use of external databases may be found only in large companies or in certain sectors of commerce. The travel trade, for instance, makes extensive use of external databases to make holiday bookings, since there can be instant checks on the availability of package holidays, flights or hotels, and reservations can be made immediately. Building societies and banks also use computer networks of various sorts to link branches together and to centralise transactions.

One example of a system which links offices together is the Clearing House Automatic Payments System (CHAPS), which has been introduced to the banking industry in Britain. CHAPS started in February 1985 and basically enabled banks to make payments to each other in the city without messengers taking pieces of paper recording transactions from one bank to another. Although by no means all banks participate in the system it does involve the four larger British banks, the two largest American banks, Citibank and the Bank of America, together with other large foreign banks like the Hong Kong and Shanghai Bank and the Swiss Bank Corporation.

Electronic mail

Electronic mail systems offer the facility for messages to be left on a terminal at a work station, to await an immediate keyboard response. Not only can individual messages be sent, but other facilities are also possible. For instance, noticeboards can be created, updated and accessed via electronic mail systems. Other possibilities are for the diaries of individuals to be checked so that meetings and appointments can be more easily scheduled. Whilst LANs may offer electronic mailing within one building, other systems offer a more widespread network over which electronic mailing can operate. One such system is the National Office System (NOS), which joins together the various locations of IBM (UK), linking the headquarters office at Portsmouth with other offices in Havant, Winchester, Basingstoke, and elsewhere in Britain. The system enables all employees to send information to each other and to correspond with colleagues in other offices instantaneously. Advanced systems of electronic mailing present further opportunities for companies to relocate away from established, and possibly congested centres. Information can be passed between individuals almost regardless of location.

New technology in retailing

Three important technological innovations have been made in the area of retailing, each of which could change quite fundamentally the way in which shops operate. One innovation is the adoption of electronic technology at the cash desk of large stores. This has brought the introduction of *Electronic point of sale* (EPOS) terminals, which allow retailers to check information from the cash desk, including details of goods sold to assist stock control and even to monitor the speed at which a particular check-out is working. A second development is the introduction of payments systems which allow the automatic transfer of money from the customer's bank account to that of the retailer. This is known as EFTPoS (*Electronic fund transfer at point of sale*). The third is the development of shopping services, often known as *teleshopping* which allow the customer to shop either from home, via a suitably equipped television set, or from a local centre, such as a local library or community centre. The last two innovations, EFTPoS and 'teleshopping', will be examined more closely, to assess what they involve and the likely implications for the future of the retail trade.

Electronic fund transfer at point of sale – EFTPoS

EFTPoS is an advanced system of payment directing money from the customer's bank account to that of the retailer. A simpler way of operating involves the use of a card which is 'charged up' with funds and is then used to pay for services. One such system is already in use by banks in France as a cash withdrawal system, whilst in Britain, the introduction of British Telecom's Phonecard for use in public telephones, uses a similar concept. Advanced EFTPoS systems, however, offer much more and have a far greater flexibility in terms of the transfer of funds. The way in which a typical advanced system operates is shown in Figure 31.

The customer offers to the cashier a card for payment, which could be a card issued by a bank or building society or a credit card, or even one issued by the retailer. The magnetic strip on the reverse of the card contains information which is scanned by a machine at the cash point. The card's details are then transmitted out of the shop via a national network to the customer's bank, building society or credit card agency. If the card is valid and funds permit, payment

An EFTPoS transaction.

is then authorised and the message is sent back to the store, along with a unique identity code. The latter is crucial, since the customer has to punch a PIN (Personal Indentification Number) on to a small numeric pad, which is linked to the check-out, as shown in the photograph on this page. Providing that the two numbers match, then payment is authorised. The payment is then transferred from the customer's account to that of the retailer. Although the information necessary to authorise the transaction will

Figure 31 Electronic fund transfer at point of sale—the sequence of events in an EFTPoS transaction

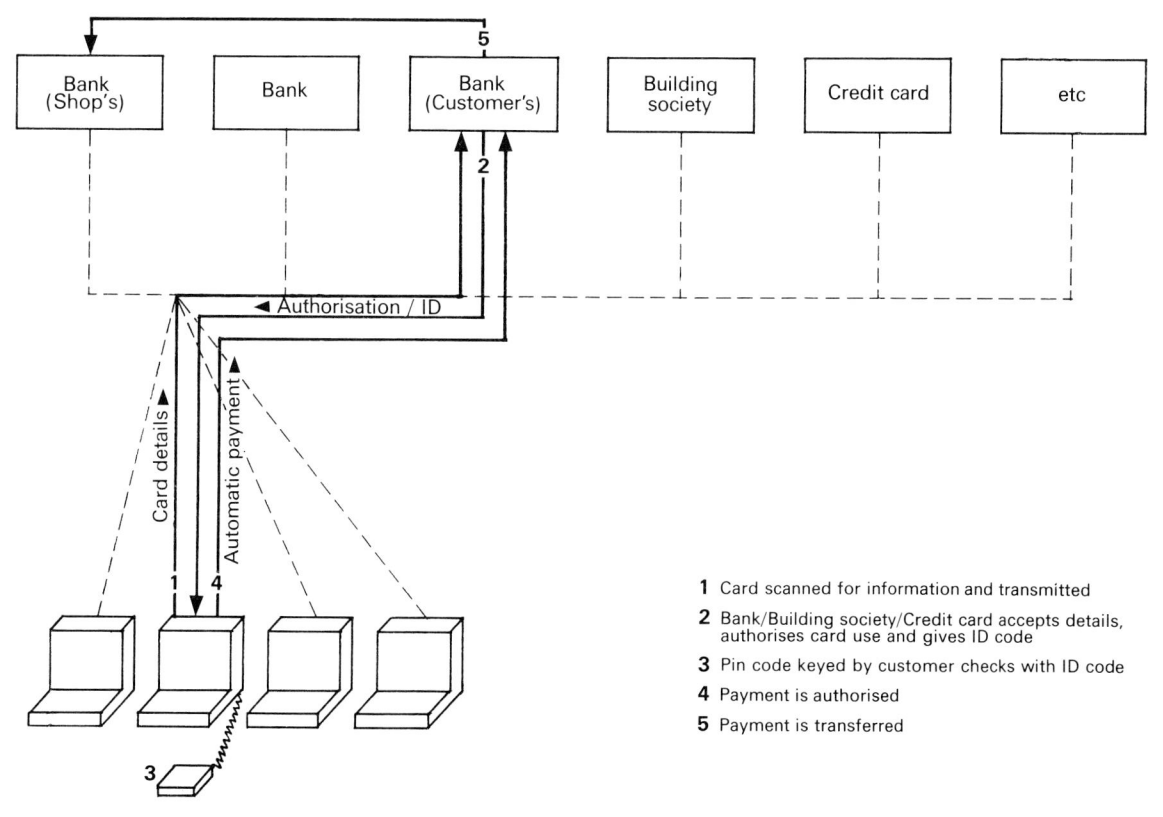

1 Card scanned for information and transmitted
2 Bank/Building society/Credit card accepts details, authorises card use and gives ID code
3 Pin code keyed by customer checks with ID code
4 Payment is authorised
5 Payment is transferred

probably have had to travel many miles, the transaction itself takes as little as ten seconds to complete.

A number of EFTPoS schemes are operating within Britain and in European countries. In France for instance, customers of a major hypermarket chain can now make their payments this way, using a card issued by the store. There are also simplified schemes for paying for petrol in French service stations using credit cards which are simply 'swiped' through a machine to authorise payment, eliminating the need for hand-written vouchers. Similar limited schemes have been started in Britain, usually on an experimental basis (McFadyen, 1986). For instance, Counterplus is a joint venture between BP Oil and Clydesdale Bank in Scotland. As early as 1982, this scheme was operating in the Aberdeen area to allow customers to pay automatically for their petrol and the system has now been made permanent.

Another larger experimental operation is that installed by the Anglia Building Society in Northampton, involving some 70 retailers. This system is known as PayPoint and operates using British Telecom lines to the headquarters of the Anglia Building Society in Northampton. The first EFTPoS scheme to use both credit cards and direct debit cards is the Midland Bank's Speedline system which was introduced in Milton Keynes in February 1986. Speedline links shops and petrol stations to a central payment system, which will accept bank automatic cash dispenser cards, such as NatWest's Servicecard, or credit cards such as Access. The scheme involves some major retailers such as C & A, Dolcis, H. Samuel and Thomas Cook, as well as BP service stations. A final example of these trial systems of EFTPoS is the DARTS (Data Capture and Authorisation Retail Transaction Service), which operates in a number of shops in the Brent Cross Shopping Centre in North London (see page 30). The scheme is operated by Barclaycard and will be expanded to accept Access, as well as charge cards such as American Express and Diners Club.

EFTPoS could considerably reduce, if not actually eliminate the handling of cash at the check-out and will generally speed up payment operations. In the process, it will cut the operation costs of retailers who will not need to employ cash clerks, or spend time in the transfer of cash to the bank. Payments will also be credited to the retailer's bank account more quickly than at present. Before that happens, however, there is obviously a need for the large financial organisations to agree on a common system, which will offer a full national network, like that suggested in Figure 31, rather than the somewhat local experiments which are currently operating.

Teleshopping

The other innovation which has perhaps more profound implications both for the location of shopping as well as for the way in which they operate is the introduction of 'teleshopping' services, or other systems which allow the customer to order goods without visiting the shop. In theory, being able to shop in this way eliminates the need for shops to be accessible to all their customers, which is in a sense an extension of the mail order system of shopping. These new schemes, however, use the new opportunities offered by interactive computer technology, with customers communicating with the retailer via a keyboard. Most of the schemes operating are still experimental, although several have been in place for some years.

Telecard Supershop is a system offered to the residents of the Richmond and Kingston areas of London. It is operated as a separate business, rather than being linked to a major conventional retailer. Customers can order goods, including fresh foodstuffs, at any time of day and up to a month in advance. There is a minimum charge and goods are delivered to the home. A second scheme operates in the Bradford area of West Yorkshire. This is Bradford Centrepoint, which is the result of collaboration with a local retailer, Morrisons Superstores. Orders are placed at terminals which are located in local community centres, libraries, centres for the disabled and similar locations, with the intention of serving as many people as possible from the one point. For those who cannot reach the terminal, ordering clerks will visit their homes to take their shopping orders. Orders are transmitted via the company's headquarters to a local store, which then delivers the goods on the following day, payment being made at the time of delivery.

The Centrepoint system follows closely the earlier system which was set up in Gateshead as a joint venture between Tesco, Gateshead (then) Metropolitan Borough Council and the University of Newcastle-upon-Tyne (Davies, 1982). This operates in much the same way with videotex TV receivers installed in local centres, although some are also in private houses. The system is deliberately restricted to those who have difficulty in reaching a conventional Tesco store. The Social Services department has been involved in the scheme and housebound customers can phone orders through to that department, for them to be placed on the system.

Use of the ordering system is restricted to relatively slack times in the store and the goods are delivered directly to the customer's home. The system has met with some problems because of the bottlenecks which occur in any major store towards the end of the week.

Since assistants have to go around the store collecting the items ordered, busy times have to be avoided if possible. The problems can be decreased by off-peak ordering, and by limiting the number of people registered to use the system, but it is clear that there are limits to such systems if they are linked to conventional superstores or hypermarkets which have peak and slack times. A separate automated warehouse would be a more workable alternative if open access were to be allowed at any time of day.

If such systems were to become more widespread then many of the disadvantaged groups, including the elderly, infirm, lower paid and non-car-owning could avail themselves of all the advantages of large scale shopping which the rest of the community are able to enjoy. More generally, they do open the way to shopping from the home via the television set, rendering in theory at least, the location of the shop irrelevant for the individual shopper. Remote purchasing of goods is not likely, however, to take over from more conventional shopping, since for most people, it is in itself a recreative and social pastime. A visit to the shops or a large store, enabling detailed comparisons to be made between goods in a pleasant atmosphere, is an activity which many people would not want to forego.

The future

Technological innovation in the office and in the shop is certainly changing the way in which people work in both areas. Many of the more tiresome tasks are being eliminated and people are being freed to do other more interesting work. At the same time, the number of people required in the service sector may well decrease over the next few years. EFTPoS and EPOS systems will both save on labour. In the case of the latter, the introduction of EPOS tills allowed a reduction in the number of check-outs from 18 to 14 at a Key Markets store in Spalding (Lincolnshire), and a reduction from 16 to 14 check-outs at a Tesco store in Edmonton (North London) (Taylor, 1984). EFTPoS will certainly lead to changes in employment in certain areas, with a reduced need for unskilled labour partly offset by an increased demand for a skilled workforce to design and maintain the new systems. It is also likely to have an effect on the labour requirements in the banking system, since the automation of payments will reduce a great deal of clerical work.

Locational considerations are also important since much of the new technology which has been introduced releases many of the locational constraints which have previously been so important to the service sector. It could be argued that increasing automation will lead to an even greater emphasis on large scale retailing, like that described in Chapter 3, but this need not necessarily be the case. Indeed there may well be a new role for the small store, since once they have been joined together into a distribution network for goods ordered from home, they offer an efficient alternative to large store operations.

The implications of new technology in shops and offices

Two major implications need to be reviewed—the effects on employment and on location. In the area of employment, there appears to be little evidence that there will be a dramatic shedding of labour as a result of the adoption of any of this new technology. There will be important shifts, however, in the type of work which is done and the sorts of skills which are required. In a general sense there will be a demand for a more skilled workforce, since the new technology is generally designed for and suited to the undertaking of routine tasks. A skilled workforce is needed to design, install, operate and maintain the new systems, whether they are in shops or offices.

Locational change is likely to take place only slowly simply on account of new technology. There are powerful social pressures which seem likely to preserve traditional shopping activities, even if the location of the shops themselves is changing. The ability to examine an article, to discuss it with a sales person and to compare goods from one shop to another is a vital part of the shopping process. Currently only those who are in the more remote regions of Britain or Europe have to shop by using remote retailing facilities—usually mail order catalogues. For the majority of people who have a choice, a visit to the shops, or the regional shopping centre is likely to be an event which is still seen as a vital social and recreational activity. In the case of office activities, current application of the available technology does little to suggest that the office worker will be able to work from home, using data transmission facilities to link home to a central office-based computer. In any event, there are social reasons for people to go to a place of work, to mix with other employees and to enjoy their company. The new technology will certainly affect where individual companies locate, but seems unlikely to lead to the disaggregation of the working office as it exists today. The office client, however, may have much to gain, since it is certainly feasible for a customer of a firm, or a major supplier to be linked directly into an electronic office for business to be conducted. This may reduce the need for personal visits, although once again, the client may wish to maintain a personal contact with the company rather than dealing with it from a keyboard.

In summary, therefore, it can safely be said that the new technology available to the service sector is having, and is likely to continue to have, a powerful influence on the way in which businesses operate. Social pressures may well determine the extent to which the full potential of the new technology is realised.

Assignments

Questions from A level examination papers

1 In what ways has the land-use pattern of the rural-urban fringe of western cities become more diversified in the last thirty years? (Associated Examining Board, June 1986)

2 To what extent do you consider the location of shops, offices and community services (such as hospitals and schools) to be influenced by considerations of the needs of the consumers? (Oxford and Cambridge, June 1983)

6
Shops and offices – where next?

It is all too easy to suggest that society either has gone, or is going through a revolution in the way in which it works. The Industrial Revolution transformed western societies as the factory system became dominant over craft-based workshops, using new sources of power which increased our society's manufacturing capability many times over. Are the changes which have been discussed in this book equally revolutionary, or are they merely part of a gradual evolution?

Department stores date back to Paris in the 1850s and have been present in major cities for the greater part of this century, so large scale retailing is hardly new. Yet a superstore in the 1980s hardly bears comparison with a department store of the 1920s. Its internal arrangement, methods and traditions of trading, and above all, its location have changed beyond recognition. In European cities, this transformation has been very swift, altering the way in which people shop in little more than 25 years. In the office, the switch has been even more rapid; 10 years ago, word processors and desk-top computers were a rarity, but now every modern office is equipped with the products of new computer technology. What is more significant for the geography of cities is that the office today is just as likely to be overlooking a parkland as it is a neighbouring multi-storey office block. Where are these trends leading?

The future of the office
The growth in some sectors of office employment may well slow down as computerisation takes care of the routine filing and other clerical tasks, which occupy so much time in the traditional office. Computer technology in various forms can easily provide a substitute for low level office skills, whilst other higher level skills involving decision-making are less easily dispensed with. The growth of financial services appears to be continuing and more and more people are going to be earning their living supporting and being supported by that sector of the economy. They in their turn will be assisted in their work by increasingly sophisticated office management systems.

City centre congestion, coupled with high rates and high land prices, may cause companies to look more carefully at their location. Some will still decide in favour of the centre with its restaurants, bars, entertainment facilities and shops which can be visited in the lunch hour by employees. For others, however, when the time comes for expansion of the company, for the installation of a new computer system requiring some structural alteration or for the expiry of a lease, possibly accompanied by a rent increase, the location of the office itself may well be reassessed. For many, the easy accessibility of a site close to a motorway, *autoroute* or *autobahn* may well be difficult to resist. If the area is also one in which highly qualified employees want to live, so much the better. The environmentally attractive regions of major countries, for example the 'Sunbelt' in the U.S. will attract companies at the expense of the older established cities.

The remote office, with the office worker sitting at a terminal in the comfort of home, whilst technically feasible, does not appear to be a likely prospect for the future. Even if the technical and cost problems of networking employees' homes with the office could be overcome, there are social reasons for people wanting to go to work, the company of colleagues and the atmosphere of the workplace being rather intangible attractions of going away from home to work. The working life of an office employee may well be transformed within the office, but it seems likely that for most people, home and work will remain physically separate.

The future of the shop
The trend towards large scale shops, in which many of the retail management tasks are increasingly automated seems inevitable. The location of many shops will become more and more peripheral since land availability dictates that pattern. Food retailing especially will follow this trend, whilst in other sectors, such as fashion, there will be a division. Some will remain in the centre, offering a wide choice for

potential customers, while others will go into new suburban regional shopping centres, such as Parly II or Brent Cross.

The emptying inner areas of cities do not have the environmental attraction which major retailers would wish to have for their smart new stores. Only very powerful incentives, such as those offered in Britain's enterprise zones, including relaxed planning controls and rates 'holidays', are really going to be sufficiently compelling to create in-town large scale retailing. On the other hand, positive planning of city centres may transform them, making them more competitive, and there are many signs of that having taken place.

The small shop, having declined so dramatically in number, may well now have a future. Many people would argue that without it, some groups in the community, especially those in rural areas, are seriously disadvantaged. Indeed a number of countries, such as Belgium, the Netherlands and Italy, have acted to safeguard the small shop. The Norwegian government saw the problem emerging, suggesting that 'a market system, steered by the free choice of consumers alone, will tend to adapt to and favour... consumers having appreciable resources at their disposal' (quoted by Kirby, 1983). In Norway, there are government management grants for shops where the population is not large enough to support the provision of one shop, as well as an investment grant to re-equip and modernise a small retail business (Kirby, 1983).

Three further trends may check the decline of the small shop. One is the introduction of the convenience store, offering a local, extended hours service, although in Britain (outside Scotland) the legal barriers to extended seven day trading, with late night opening, may stem this trend temporarily. A second possibility is for the small shop to take on a new role as a distribution centre for teleshopping, which would still allow it to act as a 'topping-up' centre for items which have been forgotten, or which are needed at short notice. A final trend is for specialist retailers to operate from small shop units. This has already begun to occur in Britain, with the emergence of new chains of shops, each specialising in one line. Examples are Sockshop and Tie Rack, both successful British ventures. Tie Rack was founded in 1981, and now has over 100 shops which are operated on a franchise basis, often sited on station concourses or busy shopping malls. Specialist small shops, responding to consumer need at convenient locations may well be a counter-trend to the increases in scale, which have been so characteristic of retailing in the recent past.

Shopping is also becoming not only a leisure pursuit, but also being linked more directly with recreational activities. The provision of sports centres in shopping centres is one trend, illustrated by the squash courts, indoor bowling and other sporting facilities which are provided in the top storey of the Eldon Square Centre in Newcastle-upon-Tyne. Other more dramatic developments have been going on elsewhere, best illustrated by the West Edmonton Mall in Canada, which has a major recreational area in one of the largest shopping developments in the world. It seems likely that similar design concepts are likely to be introduced to European cities in the near future and some plans have already been put forward for combined leisure and retail centres, such as the proposed Park Plaza development at Hatfield (Hertfordshire), which includes not only shops and offices, but also a hotel, an ice rink and a gymnasium.

Locational change

The locational shift of the service sector has taken place in a matter of decades, reshaping cities, which have taken centuries to develop. The exodus of shopping to the outskirts has been a trend in North American cities for a number of years, causing the virtual abandonment of the centre by retailers. Fortunately for European cities, the lessons from North America have been learnt and there are few signs of city centres losing retailers on a vast scale. At the same time, there are other problems in European cities, which often stem from their history. Much of the building fabric needs conservation in the face of development pressures. Old buildings have to be carefully adapted to house modern facilities, both offices and shops. Occasionally interesting solutions have been found, one example being Bath's former Green Park Station (a valued Victorian building in a predominantly Georgian city), which now houses a Sainsbury superstore. Elsewhere, however, the pressures to sweep away the old and build the new are not always resisted. The standardisation of appearance of shopping centres, with their McDonald's, Etam, C&A and Mothercare, whether they be in Cologne, Lyon or Birmingham is perhaps unfortunate, but likely to increase as retailing becomes even larger scale and more international in its organisation.

Shops and offices have changed dramatically; the pace of change, far from slowing down, is accelerating and cities and towns are having to respond to these increasing pressures. Marks and Spencer has come a long way from a stall in Leeds market in 1884 to its 94,000 sq. ft. (8,736m^2) out-of-town store in Gateshead's Metro Centre. With five more stores planned to be in edge-of-town locations by 1991, the company has moved with a trend which is now well established throughout Europe. Offices have seen no lesser change and the development of out-of-town office sites is transforming the edge of towns and cities. Journeys to work are no longer exclusively focused on the centre of the city, but have become more dispersed, with all the implications that that has for transport planning in the city. It is fair to predict that at the turn of the century the city will be very different from what it was 20 years ago. Shops and offices are undoubtedly setting the pace for this change.

Assignments

Questions from A level examination papers

1. Either: Discuss the value and limitations of any one model of city structure.
   Or: Examine the signficance of the concept of 'distance decay' to an understanding of the structure of the city. (London, January 1981)
2. 'Cities are dying.' Discuss and exemplify. (London, June 1985)
3. Show how the development of information technology may begin to affect the location of offices, shops and other community services. (Oxford and Cambridge, July 1986)
4. Why do shopping centre hierarchies develop within urban areas? (Oxford and Cambridge, July 1986)

Conclusions

Shops and offices are part of the daily lives of the majority of people in western countries—as places of work, of exchange and of social contact. As the service sector has grown in importance, so these two major functions have come to play a leading role in the way in which cities are shaped and planned. From high-rise blocks which mark the city centre, to the hypermarkets and shopping centres on the edge of the city, shops and offices give a distinctive and dynamic character to most cities. For most of this century, the traditional locational mix was one of city centre offices, with major chain and department stores in close proximity, and neighbourhood shopping scattered through the rest of the city, serving the needs of the population for their everyday goods. Much of that remains, but there have been enormous pressures for change, taking both shops and offices to locations which are peripheral to the city. Even though some countries have tried to stem this centrifugal movement, the momentum is well established and both shops and offices have undergone significant locational changes. In the process, customers, clients and workers have had to adjust to a new locational pattern. The prospects are that the adjustment will be a continual process, since the service sector is one of the most dynamic aspects of our current society.

References

Ardagh, J. (1982), *France in the 1980s* (Penguin)

Bateman, M. (1985) *Office Development: A Geographical Analysis* (Croom Helm)

Bell, D. (1973), *The Coming of Post-Industrial Society* (Heinemann)

Bennison, D. and Davies, R. L. (1977), 'The local effects of city centre shopping schemes: a case study', (paper presented to PTRC 5th Summer Annual Meeting)

Bromley, R.D.F. and Morgan, R.H. (1985), 'The effects of enterprise zone policy: evidence from Swansea', *Regional Studies*, vol. 19(5), pp. 403–414

Burtenshaw, D., Bateman, M. and Ashworth, G.J. (1981). *The City in West Europe* (John Wiley & Sons)

Daniels, P.W. (1982), *Service Industries: Growth and Location* (CUP)

Daniels, P.W. (1985), 'Producer services in the post-industrial space economy', in Martin, R. and Rowthorn, B. (eds), *Deindustrialization and the British Space Economy* (Macmillan)

Davies, R.L. (1982), 'The Gateshead Shopping and Information Service: a progress report', *Retail Planning and Development*, (Proceedings of Seminar at PTRC 10th Summer Annual Meeting), pp. 45–52

Davies, R.L. (1984), *Retail Commercial Planning* (Croom Helm)

Davies, R.L. (1985), 'Shopping centre development in Newcastle-upon-Tyne and Tyne and Wear Metropolitan County', in Dawson, J.A. and Lord, J.D., (eds), *Shopping Centre Development: Policies and Prospects* (Croom Helm)

Dawson, J.A., Burt, S.L., and Sparks, L. (1983), *Hypermarkets and Superstores: a Bibliography* (Euromonitor)

Goddard, J.B. (1973), *Office Linkages and Location: a Study of Communications and Spatial Patterns in Central London* (Pergamon)

Gottmann, J. (1970), 'Urban centrality and the interweaving of quaternary activities', *Ekistics*, pp. 129, 322–31

Husain, M. S. (1980), 'Office relocation in Hamburg: the City-Nord Project', *Geography*, vol. 65(2), pp. 131–4

Institute of Grocery Distribution (1981), *Retail Grocery Trade Review 1981* (Letchmore Heath)

Kirby, D. (1983), 'Trial and error is no way to run a small shop', *The Guardian*, 19 August 1983

Lasserre, C. (1985), 'De Europese hoofstad Brussel', (paper presented to seminar on investment in Europe, Amsterdam, 19 June 1985)

Marquand, J. (1983), 'The changing distribution of service employment', in Goddard, J.B. and Champion, A.G., (eds), *The Urban and Regional Transformation of Britain* (Methuen)

McFadyen, E. (1986), 'EFTPoS: The urgent need for standardisation', *Retail and Distribution Management*, May/June 1986, pp. 30–32

Newby, P.T. and Shepherd, I.D.H. (1979), 'Brent Cross: a milestone in retail development', *Geography*, vol. 64, pp. 133–7

Percival, G. (1985), 'Who's next out of town?', *Estates Gazette*, 12 October 1985, pp. 150–52

Taylor, A. (1984), 'The planning implications of new technology in retailing and distribution', *Town Planning Review*, vol. 55(2), pp. 161–76

Tuppen, J. (1977), 'Redevelopment of the City Centre: the case of Lyon—La Part Dieu', *Scottish Geographical Magazine*, vol. 93(3), pp. 151–8

Index

accessibility 6, 11–12, 28, 30, 53
agglomeration 11
anchor stores 27–8
ASDA Superstores 16, 18, 23, 24, 25

banking 2, 3
bid rent theory 11–12
Brent Cross (London) 28, 30, 54
business parks 9, 42–3

Canary Wharf (London) 43–4
car ownership 6, 20, 31
centralisation 35
Centres E. Leclerc 23
City Nord (Hamburg) 38–9
Coin Street (London) 38
consumer services 2
contact environment 6
convenience stores 27, 54
corner shop 20
Créteil Soleil (Paris) 29–30

deconcentration 6, 7, 35
deindustrialisation 2
department stores 6, 7, 19, 22, 28, 53
deregulation (of financial markets) 36, 44
Docklands (London) 7, 43–4

Eastgate Centre (Basildon) 30–4
EFTPoS 48–50
Eldon Square (Newcastle-upon-Tyne) 28, 34, 54
electronic mail 48
electronic office 47–8
employment change 2–3, 7, 51
enterprise zones 17, 43, 54

European Economic Community 8

financial institutions 15, 28
financial services 3, 44, 53
foreign banks 35–6

Green Belts 25, 28

Habitat 21, 22
hypermarkets 6, 23–5

independent retailers 19, 20
information technology 34
inner city 17, 21
insurance 2, 3
insurance companies 15–16

La Défense (Paris) 40–41
land use theory 9, 11–14
land values 11–12, 14
La Part Dieu 28, 39–40
local area networks (LANs) 47–8
local community 38, 44
local planning 17, 25
Location of Offices Bureau (LOB) 37
Loi Royer 25

mail order 51
Marks and Spencer plc 20, 22, 28, 30
Metro Centre (Gateshead) 28
métropoles d'equilibre 4
Mothercare 21, 22
motorways 12, 37

new towns 29
Norly 2 (Lyon) 43

Office Development Permits (ODPs) 36
office location 36–45

office parks – see business parks
office technology 9, 46–8

Parly II (Paris) 29, 54
pension funds 15–16
planning controls 25–7
planning process 17, 38
primary activities 1
producer services 2, 3
property development 9, 15, 38
property market 14–16

quaternary sector 1
quinary sector 2

regional employment variation 3–6
regional shopping centres 27–34, 39
retailing changes 21–3
retail warehouses 27

St Sever (Rouen) 28
Schéma Directeur d'Aménagement Urbain 17
secondary activities 1
service sector 1, 2, 4, 7
Storehouse plc 21
structure plans 17
superstores 6, 23–5

teleshopping 50–1, 54
tertiary sector – see service sector
Tesco Stores Ltd 18, 21, 50
transport 11, 12

voluntary retail groups 19

Windmill Hill (Swindon) 42–3
word processors 48, 53
work stations 47–9